Emotional

C000099889

How to Stop Procrastination and Rewire Your Brain

(Boosting Your Social Skills for Leadership)

Marie E. Domitrovich

Published by Kevin Dennis

Marie E. Domitrovich

All Rights Reserved

Emotional Intelligence: How to Stop Procrastination and Rewire Your Brain (Boosting Your Social Skills for Leadership)

ISBN 978-1-989965-25-2

Legal & Disclaimer

The information contained in this book is not designed to replace or take the place of any form of medicine or professional medical advice. The information in this book has been provided for educational and entertainment purposes only.

The information contained in this book has been compiled from sources deemed reliable, and it is accurate to the best of the Author's knowledge; however, the Author cannot guarantee its accuracy and validity and cannot be held liable for any errors or omissions. Changes are periodically made to this book. You must consult your doctor or get professional medical advice before using any of the suggested remedies, techniques, or information in this book.

TABLE OF CONTENTS

Introduction

Everything you've done up to this point has made you who you are and has accounted for many defining moments in your life. It is the integration of all these that has formed the totality of behavior, characteristics and idiosyncrasies that make up your personality. Yet, somewhere along the way, we have learned to hide the hardships we faced, the blemishes and scars we got and the obstacles we had to scale to get where we are. So, it is safe to say that in this game of charades called life, everyone shows the photoshopped version of their personalities. This is why most business owners don't really tell you about their experiences back when they were just starting up.

We've all been through different circumstances and situations that have allowed us to blossom or understand things we may have not been able to understand before – different eureka moments that have proved critical in the progress of our lives and these moments would not have been recognized or identified without at least a basic understanding of our

Chapter 1: History Of Emotional Intelligence

A book "Frames of Mind: The Theory of Multiple Intelligences" written by Howard Gardner published in 1983. The book introduced the idea of traditional types, including IQ and failure to elucidate cognitive ability. The book explained the basic concepts of multiple intelligences, including interpersonal and intrapersonal aptitude.

Interpersonal Intelligence: It is an aptitude to recognize the intentions, stimulus and wishes of other people.

Intrapersonal Intelligence: It is an aptitude to understand others to appreciate their mindset, qualms and motivations.

EMOTIONAL CAPITAL MODEL OF EMOTIONAL INTELLIGENCE

A study was conducted in 1985 by Wayne Payne to understand the emotional intelligence. In 1990s, the "Emotional Intelligence" was described as a form of social intelligence that describes the ability to monitor emotions and feelings of another person. Salovey and Mayer had started a research program to develop suitable procedures to determine the emotional intelligence and its implication. They did research on one group of people and observe their emotions while viewing a sad movie. The people with good score with emotional clarity came out of their upset emotions more quickly. These people were able to respond athletically to bring adjustments in their social environment and networks.

Daniel Goleman and Emotional Intelligence

The Daniel Goleman noticed the work of Salovey and Mayer in 1990s and ultimately started his own book "Emotional Intelligence". He wrote science articles in the New York Times and specialized in brain and behavior research. He was a psychologist at Harvard and worked with David McClelland, a group of researchers. Some traditional tests were conducted to test cognitive intelligence. The Goleman argued that cognitive intelligence is not or business success, but to describe emotional intelligence. Emotional intelligence is described by the four characteristics:

Self-awareness (Good understanding of personal emotions)

Self-management (Good management of personal emotions)

Social Awareness (Compassionate to the emotional drivers to other people)

Social Skills (good handling of other's emotions)

Emotional intelligence of Goleman proved that the term is more important than the IQ. The book was best-selling book, but it also received criticism in terms of leadership and business success.

The Mayer and Salovey list some branches of Emotional Intelligence in their publication of 1997. They arrange a physiological study and explain some branches to recognize and articulate emotions. The four branches of Emotional Intelligence are:

Perception Appraisal and Expression of Emotion

Emotional Facilitation of Thinking

Understand and analyze emotions through emotional knowledge

Reflect regulations for emotions and promote intellectual growth

Chapter 2: Key Benefits

Life is all about relationships. And relationships are built on emotions. So naturally, becoming self-aware and therefore controlling your emotions is vital in having success both in your personal and professional life. I've compiled a list of benefits across all aspects of life so you get an idea of how Emotional Intelligence can improve the quality of your life:

Self-Control: Emotions are triggered by external events therefore it's natural to react to things in a destructive way if negative emotions are trigged. For example, a natural reaction to an employee making a mistake could be that you start to point out their mistakes more than you praise their good work, leading to low motivation and lowered productivity in the workforce; a vicious circle seen in many business environments. Being able to take yourself out of the situation and look at the bigger picture means you could react in a positive manner, ensuring your employee respects you and is more motivated to not make mistakes, meaning your business is more productive in the long run.

Self-control also covers the ability to endure delayed gratification. This is the ability to endure sacrificing short term comforts now for the vision of success in the long term. Emotional intelligence means although you may want to give up or procrastinate now because you feel stressed or upset, looking at the bigger picture and realizing how you could feel later on if you stick to it gives you emotional control and self-control over your actions, along with the motivation to keep going.

The famous Stanford Marshmallow experiment gave children a choice between being given one marshmallow right away, or waiting for a short amount of time and being given two. They found that the children who opted to wait and receive two marshmallows had higher success rates in school and their careers later on than those who opted for the one marshmallow. These children most likely grew up in emotionally intelligent environments, perhaps learning it from their parents.

Self-Motivation: Similar to self-control, being self-aware of your emotions is vital to staying on track with your goals and working productively towards them. A lot of people get distracted by short term comforts such as social media meaning they do not get as much work done throughout the working day. Simply looking at the bigger picture, you can understand that although short term bursts of pleasure are good, delayed gratification leads to better chances of success down the road. Thinking like this means you are far more likely to put in the work now, being happy in the knowledge that the hard work you put in now will pay off later. Being assured of your own abilities will also increase self-confidence which overlaps with social skills too.

Stress Management: Being self-aware means you understand that stress is simply caused by your own perception of a situation (usually people's perceptions are blown up due to the negative emotions controlling them, causing bad decisions to be made). Assessing the positives and negatives of a situation means you're in check with what needs to be done to resolve the situation. Being in control even under pressure means you will never have to get hung up on stress again.

Mental and Physical health: Stress management naturally means a peaceful mind and a healthy body. Stress can cause all sorts of health problems such as high blood pressure and cardiovascular disease. Furthermore, lowering stress and being able to control emotions to develop a positive outlook on life means you are less likely to let negative emotions take over long term and cause mental health issues such as anxiety and depression. Emotional intelligence boosts self-confidence and motivation meaning you will actively work to maintain a healthy mind, body, soul and heart.

Leadership Skills: Emotionally intelligent people are able to inspire others and can make great decisions quickly, meaning they are great leaders. In order to lead a team, you must be able to understand and help with their needs; if you can do that you can inspire them to work towards a common goal and that is invaluable in business growth. Being able to control emotions and not base decisions on negative emotions, whilst also evaluating the positives and negatives of an outcome means quick and informed decisions can be made to move a project in the right direction.

Decision Making: Your life is moulded by your everyday decisions. Simply put, deciding to work out for 30 minutes every morning will over time create a healthy, energetic, low stress and happier lifestyle. Deciding to lie in bed instead and eat junk food to save time will, over time, create an unhealthy, low energy, depressive lifestyle. It's the small decisions you make that don't seem like they mean a lot that eventually lead you to success, or to failure. That's why basing decisions on logical, educated thoughts rather than current emotions (which could either be positive or negative) is imperative to success. Being self-aware of your emotional state and controlling it means making smarter decisions.

It has been found that emotionally intelligent people are not effected by anxiety when making decisions, but people with low emotional intelligence are influenced by anxiety in their decision making.

Social Skills: Networking is key in business, and as they say, 'business is built on relationships'. Therefore, being able to influence the emotions of others will help hugely in growing your circle and developing productive relations. Social skills are also key to making new personal friends so social skills help in every aspect of life.

Relationship Management: This is similar to social skills but on a more personal level. Happiness depends a lot on our relationships so building/maintaining deep and long lasting relationships with partners/spouses/family is vital to leading a happy life. Being able to use empathy to influence the emotions of others will provide a core tool to ensuring relationships stay happy and conflict is always resolved or avoided.

As you can see, emotional intelligence is applicable to all walks of life: starting within us in maintaining a healthy mind and body, leading to external relationships both personally and professionally. Developing Emotional Intelligence will truly allow us to become the masters of our own minds and will help us succeed in all walks of life. With the internal/external peace and confidence developed through emotional intelligence, we will be well on our way to achieving successful and most importantly HAPPY lives.

Conflict Management: There's a lot of optimistic and happy people in this world that are very easy to get along with. Unfortunately, there are also a lot of negative people who just seem to want to argue at the slightest trigger. Perhaps even you have days where you argue a lot because you're stressed or sad about something. Emotional intelligence comes into play in these moments, allowing you to snub conflict before it blows up by changing your own emotional state and influencing others' emotional states positively.

Chapter 3: Why Emotional Intelligence

Matters

There is a reason that people who succeed often have average-to-high levels of emotional intelligence. Even though there is no predisposition that determines a person's emotional intelligence, EQ plays a critical role in a person's success. IQ cannot predict it, nor can an individual's personality. However, together, these three things form a trifecta that can be used to help predict a person's inclination toward success.

Of these three characteristics, emotional intelligence is the easiest to change. IQ merely describes your full potential for learning, which is not something that can be taught. People who test their IQ at 15 have the same IQ as they would at 50. So, if you want to boost success, it only makes sense to turn to the other contributing factors. While you cannot necessarily change your personality, you can change the characteristics that go alone with it.

Before you even consider this, however, you need to be able to manage your emotions and control your actions. You achieve this through emotional intelligence.

Emotional intelligence matters because it determines how successful you can be. Like having a low IQ can possibly limit someone's abilities, having low emotional success prevents you from making the actions and interacting with people in a way that encourages success.

Benefits of Mastering Emotional Intelligence

People do not necessarily like change. It is common for people to become stagnant because they want to stay in their comfort zones and exist where they are most familiar. While this seems like a nice way to live life, it actually holds you back from growing and becoming successful.

Even so, most people need incentive to change. This especially true when making a change in the area of emotional intelligence. It is a change that is going to take a significant amount of time, so people who are successful are usually those who have a clear picture of what they are getting out of it. Here are the skills that emotional intelligence can help you develop:

1. Heightened Emotional Awareness

One thing that psychologists have learned is that the way people respond in certain situations stems from their emotions. Thus, if you can learn to control your reactions to these emotions, you ultimately gain a greater control of your actions than someone who is not emotionally intelligent. This means you are less likely to act irrationally. For example, you might be inclined to talk to your boss after a meeting if you felt like he disregarded your comments and get important feedback, rather than storming around the office all day in a negative, unproductive mindset.

2. Increased Self-Confidence

Another common trait that people with high emotional intelligence have is a higher level of self-confidence. Self-confidence is key to success because it gives you the courage to learn from your mistakes instead of beating yourself up over them. Additionally, it helps you know what your abilities are and what you are capable of, which can help propel you toward a higher version of success.

3. Greater Self-Control

Have you ever acted out of emotion, instead of evaluating the situation first to decide what you should do about it? This is a common occurrence, particularly for people who are not in touch with their emotional intelligence. If you have ever been cut off in traffic and reacted with anger, possibly honking your horn or letting out a string of obscenities, then you understand how those sudden emotional impulses can make you act without thinking.

Instead, in the situation above, it's important to realize that the person has already cut you off, so there is nothing you can change. Feeling angry about it just invites negative, toxic, unhelpful feelings into your life. Instead, it would make more sense to think about the reason that the person may have cut you off—maybe they needed to change lanes and only had a small window before their turn or maybe they were rushing to the hospital to see a loved one who had been hurt. It is much healthier to think of the incident this way, instead of reacting out in anger, when all the anger does is harm your own mood.

4. Increased Trustworthiness

When you are in touch with your emotional intelligence, your relationships with people will change. They will start to see you as someone that upholds standards of integrity and honesty. This leads to them feeling as if they can trust you more.

These feelings also transform into a sense of conscious. You become aware of yourself and your actions and learn to accept responsibility for them in your life. This also increases control, since you realize that the way you respond to life's circumstances ultimately determines the scenarios that happen and what is going on in your life.

5. Better Adaptability

Even people who consider themselves at the peak of success are going to experience setbacks and unexpected circumstances in life. These types of scenarios often have a slew of negative emotions and worries attached to them. Feeling badly about them, however, does not give you the chance to deal with the problem at all. It invites negative feelings into your life that inhibit your ability to handle the scenario that caused the emotions to begin with.

Emotional intelligence gives you the ability to handle these unexpected circumstances. Rather than going through the throes of emotion that come along with unpleasant situations, you can focus your mental efforts on analyzing the emotions and then decide how to act. This saves valuable time, especially in scenarios when your decision making needs to happen quickly.

6. Increased Innovation

Sometimes, the emotional side of your mind shoots down ideas before your rational mind has a chance to evaluate them. The decreases innovation and creativity, often because it invokes feelings of fear or worry about the idea not working. Once you develop greater emotional intelligence, you can intercept these thoughts from your emotional mind. This lets you tap into the creative side of your mind, particularly in problem solving scenarios.

7. Greater Commitment

Emotional intelligence gives you the confidence to keep a certain goal in your sights, regardless of how challenging it may be. This comes not only from self-confidence, but also from a drive toward achievement. When you obtain emotional intelligence, you realize that there is always a higher standard that you can achieve. This lets you set your goals higher. Additionally, once you do set your sights on a task, it helps you commit to it.

8. Improved Drive and Motivation

Two of the most important things regarding motivation is clear goals and the positive attitude that will help you get it done. This is the biggest driving factor in success—is the ability to take the actions that you need to achieve goals in your life. You cannot sit around and wish that things were better, you have to have the motivation to achieve it. Emotionally intelligent people not only know this, they have the drive to try and do better.

9. Increased Positivity in Life

Optimism is not something that means woefully ignoring what is in front of you. Being positive is about having the strength of mind to know that life is not all about setbacks. It is knowing that there are times when things may seem negative or that things are out of your control, but still persisting forward anyway. Those with high emotional intelligence do not avoid problems—but they accept them as a natural part of life and use their positivity as the backbone that helps them overcome the setbacks and obstacles that stand in their way.

10. Increased Empathy and Understanding

When dealing with others, having the ability to understand your own emotions and intentions can give you some insight into theirs as well. Having high emotional intelligence is not just about being able to relate to the things you know, however. People with high emotional intelligence understand that they do not know everyone's perceptions, feelings, and situations in the world. This makes them better because they are empathetic to situations they cannot understand. This can help greatly in relationships.

Empathy also lets you understand the signals that people send out more clearly, giving you a clearer picture of their intentions and what they really hope to gain from the interaction. This is useful in your personal relationships, but also in the workforce. Once you gain a clearer picture of what your boss or clients want, then you have a better chance of fulfilling their expectations.

11. Helping Others Progress

When you develop a deeper understanding of others, you also develop a deeper understanding of the things they need to succeed in life. This could be an emotional success, like achieving greater happiness, or overcoming something that is holding them back. As you have a better understanding of the needs of people around you, you can use this to help deepen your relationship and bolster their abilities.

This works on an interpersonal level, as well in interpersonal relationships. Having a clear understanding of an employee's needs, skills, and shortcomings, lets you encourage greater success. This relates to your own success and the success of the company that you work for (or own).

12. Better Leadership and Team Capabilities

When you can use emotional intelligence for better communication and understanding, you can learn to work better in a team and as a leader. This includes bringing groups together to pursue similar goals, working with others toward a shared goal, and persuading effectively when needed. These things make it easy to succeed in social setting, as well as in the workplace.

13. Increased Social Skills

Social skills are one of the key parts of emotional intelligence because it is not enough to understand your own emotions—you must be able to understand the emotions of others and use them to determine a course of action. Social skills include things like conflict management, which helps with negotiations and resolution of disagreements. Other social skills include building bonds and nurturing relationships, communicating more clearly, and being able to initiate change when it is needed.

14. Improved Mental Health

When you understand your emotions more, it will improve your mental health. It may make your thinking more positive and give you a clearer head when dealing with obstacles in life. You will also be able to understand your feelings better, which gives you the opportunity to find a solution. Additionally, the improved quality of the relationships that you have can create more positive feelings in your life.

15. Better Quality of Life

People with high emotional intelligence have the skills that they need to have a better quality of life. They have enough self-confidence to go after their goals and the ability to understand their own needs. They also have better relationships, which improves their level of enjoyment. In the next chapter, we'll discuss techniques you can use to develop these skills and increase your EQ.

Chapter 4: How To Control Your Emotion

And Make A Success Of Everything!

Feeling is important element of your daily life; as you desire you are able to communicate it. Creating great utilization of your feeling is actually a life worth living although you will be emotional. Express achieve success that is greater and your feeling appropriately.

You can attain success that is higher; you can obtain better success by way of a driving force stated in your world of trigger. As you activate your sensible and reasonable mind take your tips as true. Trigger the process of creating reassurance through awareness, repetition guided and Emotional ideas that are well mixed.

Because it proceeds on the prediction of truth of every idea take overall control over the emotion which reaches your mind, reason. Produce a reasoning process which exhibit the excellence of this fact in accord using the feelings associated with it so you often lead yourself to your reliable wealth, knowledge, accomplishment and abundance.

Have self-control and do things right at the appropriate moment. Have mission control that is an ideal definition of the suitable objective statement without declaring a word, while you create affirmation.

This is time to have powerful, large-wrought emotion that compels to activity because of the fact that issues are currently becoming better and will generally progress.

Spark the hearth, desire, power of conviction and the travel you must control yourself towards achieving your vision. Let the things that drives your economic and societal motor overlap your achievements. Be brave, comprehensive, sensitive, important, positive, affirming, complicated, encouraging fearless - focused. Have sense of humor when you obtain higher success and trust.

Secure your Emotional power-on subjective and beneficial response of the desiring state of well-being that enhances your effective state. Improve your frame of mind that assents for the excellent living! Be saturated in love and boost your way of pointing your forcefulness that is psychological. Successfully manage your largewrought feeling that persuade to action and be productive. Have abnormal individuality and increase of being securely mounted on a global that filled with greater living, your experienced state. Have total reassurance regarding the impact inside your world of contact's fact.

Observe how influential you're and start to become extremely powerful. See the best-in you and genuinely believe that just the greatest is adequate for you. Start to see the best-in others and bring the top inside them out.

Regardless of how Emotional perhaps you are, change your Emotional force toward achieving achievement that is greater in everything.

Controlling our thoughts is just a challenge in today's moment, especially for most folks. There are numerous facets which are inclined to bother our emotions. A partner doesn't seem to answer favorably to us. A young child wants to do his factor and we get angry. Her garbage includes in our yard and we should chuck it back to her property.

What most of us don't know is that emotions possess a greater root than just our hormones, our actual or emotional make up. There's without it being realized by people an interior heart who will bother our Emotional balance. This character leads us to overlook factors or do items which we might regret down the road and makes our internal soul excited.

Below then are recommendations on taming an over excited intrinsic character who makes discrepancy in our emotional reaction to the things, phrases or actions around us.

1. Be Convinced that Feelings Are Controlled

You've to become certain first that emotions are controllable, if you prefer to regulate your sensations. You take them and are able to handle. it can be carried out using the appropriate perspective in life's growth although the taming of an emotion may not occur quickly.

The certainty that feelings can be managed is essential with their management.

Some people believe that there are emotions which Can 't be managed. They offer the illustration of grief or sadness' emotion. Each time a person dear to us dies, based on them, we cannot help but be cry depressing, grief-stricken, weep. But I've witnessed situations upon scenarios of individuals who do not display the emotion of despair or disappointment at the death of the loved one. In such cases consequently folks do manage their feeling of suffering. Or even this emotion is not present.

I've visited funerals where not there is just a tear shed. Individuals attending the funeral and funeral rites, fresh and aged, do not sport an experience that is miserable. They respond in a, serious way that is normal, respecting the customs employed.

I have participated in the burial rituals of Adventist and Baptist Christians. These did not cry, once we discover usually in Catholic funerals and burials. People are not unable to control their emotions. You too could handle your thoughts.

The character who is our foe insinuates that we can't control our feelings. And he is believed by many of us. We get excited over a loved one's demise. Simply tell this character that one may manage your emotions, whether they are of despair, dread, dislike or other emotions.

2. Enhance Equanimity's Soul in Every Areas of Your Lifetime

How do you develop equanimity, that character of calmness and being eventempered on all instances? By stepping into the practice of experiencing the perspective the product or physical points we observe us around are merely transferring our method. They are momentary. They never withstand. They don't last forever.

Human beings expire into another container or the grave and get old and soon are forgotten. other creatures and also our pets also get their way. The towns around us may eventually become lots of aluminum and stones, as happened previously with all the renowned cities in the past. The trees around us burned by wildfire, can be shared by acid rain, or washed by erosion towards the seas.

Nothing except the Absolute Spirit and our tones are lasting.

The feeling of sadness as we bid ultimate farewell to some dying person is stirred within me after I am hoping for your dying. But I-say to myself, this also may perish. And grief's feeling is cast away. When I am fearful in the dark, I-say to myself, this may also pass away.

However, you must get this a behavior. If you are confronted by a solid feeling or even an irrational response, like an ensuing burst of frustration, just tell yourself, "This also may expire." Once you get enthusiastic over earning in a lottery say, "This also will perish". When you're currently seeing a boxing round and you feel excited since your desired boxer is all about to knockdown his adversary, just claim with focus around the meaning of the language, "This also may expire."

Growing this pattern can overcome that overexcited heart who wants to disrupt you and possibly trigger your heart failure or a stroke.

3. Be Grateful For the Nature of Interior and Calmness Happiness

Within the final reckoning Emotional control is just a surprise of Absolutely The Spirit. He wishes you to be happy and satisfied, not to be emotionally unbalanced and overexcited. Consequently, he offers you of his or her own heart of equanimity and peace. Regular fellowship with him infuses inner joy into your psyche and you dwell with energy to ward off all control of the unruly character over you.

Chapter 5: The Source Of Emotion's

A person can never achieve his or her maximum potential if emotions are not managed properly. In this regard, emotional management means that we are capable of choosing our actions even in the face of strong emotions.

All the emotions programmed in our minds are designed to make us act fast toward a certain stimuli. When there is a dangerous animal present in the vicinity, our fear will make us run for safety.

If we are angry, we tend to clench our fist as if we are ready to fight. These are automatic responses that humans developed to deal with environmental dangers. They are our reflexes and they are very useful survival mechanisms.

However, not all the survival mechanisms that prehistoric man developed are useful in our current way of living. When a child meets a new teacher, he is naturally anxious. He may even feel genuine fear towards the teacher. Though he feels fear, he is expected to face the situation and get school tasks done.

Adults have the same experience when they go out of their comfort zone. However, they are better equipped in dealing with emotions, making them in control of their actions. Yet, we still allow emotions to get the best of us. Road rage is an excellent example of this.

An emotionally intelligent person knows when to follow his or her emotions and when to override the default reactions that come with these emotions. To become emotionally intelligent, you will do best to learn about the true purpose of common emotions and your default reactions towards them.

Becoming aware for your own thought processes is a crucial part of learning how to manage your emotions, along with paying attention of your mood changes and how your emotions affect your thoughts. If you become aware of these things, you will have the power to change the way your mind deals with emotions.

This power will lead to a balanced mind; an emotional equilibrium.

The balance between the brain and the heart

An emotionally intelligent person has a balanced state of mind. He or she knows when to use the mind to make decisions and when to use emotions as a guide in choosing an action. Your balanced approach towards managing your emotions will ultimately have a positive effect in your productivity and your relationships.

If you achieved a balance between your mind and your emotions, you are the one in control of your actions. For example, you do not let small things make you angry. You are aware of your anger but you choose not to act on it because it can cause more harm than good in your relationships. This is an example of the battle between your heart and your mind.

We usually refer to the heart as the source of our emotions. However, the heart is not responsible for them. They come from our brain. It comes from a part of our brain that we have little control over.

As mentioned above, emotions exist to invoke a specific action from us. These impulsive actions are important for situations where there is no time to think and analyze. Many psychologists refer to this part of the brain as our reptilian brain.

You may think that the intelligent and rational part of your mind is in control of your actions. However, most of the time, it is our reptilian brain that gets its way. This part of our brain is called the basal ganglia. It makes us act based on our survival instincts.

The basal ganglia makes us stop whatever we are doing when we are hungry and look for food. It makes us take a nap when we are sleepy. It controls our actions by making us feel emotions.

Not all of the emotions that our reptilian brain makes us feel are necessary. Some people are prone to becoming angry for unimportant reasons because their reptilian brain is conditioned to use anger to cope with unexpected negative circumstances. Though anger becomes a habit for these people, they can override it if they become aware of how their mind works.

The more logical part of your brain or the cerebral neocortex allows you to think rationally. This part exists to tame the reptilian brain and this is the part of the mind that is considered to be the conscious part of who we are. This is where we think about our plans and the other things that make us a functioning member of the society.

You may ask why there are a lot of times when reason does not prevail over our emotions. This happens because our reptilian brain is the dominant factor that causes our behavior. The intelligent and rational part of our brain, the cerebral neocortex, must convince our basal ganglia that overriding our emotions is the right call.

We are constantly experiencing the struggle for power of these two parts of our brain. When we feel too lazy to get up from work, it is our reptilian brain talking.

When we do summon the strength to get up and start our day, our rational side has successfully convinced our primitive side.

When we go back to bed for a short nap, even when we do not need one, it means that our rational side lost the battle and the primitive side won.

This may make you think that our primitive side is preventing us to become successful. However, our reptilian brain still exists today because it is an important factor in our survival. There are times when our primitive mind must triumph over our logical mind.

For instance, when faced with starvation, it is common for parents to miss a meal to be able to feed their offspring. This is not very logical. The parents should eat more than the children because it is they who look for food. They need more energy than their young. However, their parental instincts make them willing to sacrifice their meals to increase the chance of survival of their offspring.

Chapter 6: The Subject Line – (Managing Self)

A few months ago, I received an email from someone whose name I did not recognize, with a subject line of "Can't wait to catch up with you". At first glance, the subject is benign and should not cause any alarm. But, if you, like me get a bunch of spam it looks like just another attempt for some dating or mating organization trying to solicit business. These emails are tawdry and become increasingly annoying. That one made it into the virtual trash bin. Then a few days later, I got an email from the same person with a subject line of FW: Can't wait to catch up with you. That email joined its predecessor. I continued to ignore the emails from this person until finally the subject line read, "Follow up from our CCT meeting in June."

The sender, Susan, happened to be a wonderful person I met at a coaching community meeting. When I met her, I was told her married name, but her emails had her maiden name, so I did not recognize it. and I would have blocked her permanently from my mail if I did not recognize her name. I was introduced to her by her married name and her email had her maiden name. Subsequently, we have connected and we both would have lost out if we did not connect initially due to a cryptic subject line.

Make your subject lines work for you and help the recipient respond appropriately. The subject line should indicate the topic and what action the recipient should take. Here are some effective subject lines:

Minutes of 1/15/2011 meeting – please note action items

Proposal you requested – please reply by 1/30/2011

Break through ideas – please rank by importance.

FYI only – No action required.

I strongly advocate using a person's name in the salutation but please don't use it in the subject line as it is inappropriate and considered rude especially if the recipient of the email is your business superior. In the business world when sending a note to multiple individuals, it may not be possible to use a person's name in the subject line but if you are communicating with just one person, use the person's name when it makes sense.

Jeanne, For your information only.

Jeanne, FYI only, No action required.

Jeanne Please read in preparation for the XYZ meeting.

Jeanne, please respond by Date

Jeanne, Your input please ?.

When I open my email in-box, I scan through the scores of emails I receive daily and delete a bunch of them before I attempt to open any of them. I delete the emails if I don't trust the source or if the subject line reads Fw: Fw: Fw: Fw Fw.

When an email is replied to repeatedly, it carries the subject line of the original note. You may want to consider changing or updating the subject line if the context of your most current note has changed from the original subject line. Consider and craft your subject lines to intrigue, inform and get the response you require.

Chapter 7: Developing Charisma

So here's the thing: Could charisma really be developed? Or, is it something inborn? While not everyone has charisma right away, it does not mean it could no longer be developed. According to the **American Psychological Association** (APA), people who know how to endure hardship, and who are willing to improve themselves can develop charisma—especially when they're willing to have a positive outlook in life.

Take note that charisma is not automatically linked with physical beauty—and that's why you could do so much about it. It's not about changing your whole personality, but rather about trying to improve yourself so that you'd have the X-Factor—and so doors of opportunities would open up for you.

Read on and find out how you could help yourself develop some charisma!

Body Language and Presence

First up is developing presence, and knowing proper body language. These are deemed to be important aspects of one's personality. Even without saying a word, having the right body language could help you exude likability and warmth.

Presence, meanwhile, is all about you making sure that you are attentive enough. In a classroom for example, you might notice that there are people who go to class, and who are physically present—but are mentally absent. And guess what? No one wants to be around those kinds of people for the sole reason that it's like being with a robot. And even if the world today has all these modern items, it's still best to be with people who have hearts—and who knows how to give attention not only to themselves, but also to others.

Exercises

Here are some exercises that you could try in order to develop proper body language and presence.

Practice the right body language.

For starters, this means standing up straight, making sure your head and your back are up, and making open movements. This will make people realize you're willing to talk to them, and that you are not holding back.

Be animated.

When talking to people, try to make it seem as if you are telling them a story, and that you are not lecturing them. Smile with your eyes! Be natural.

Avoid the following mannerisms:

touching your face, shifting your weight from side to side, playing with your fingers, touching your ears, putting hands in your pockets, arranging clothes over and over again, crossing the arms, pacing back and forth, **and** adjusting your hair.

Practice Active Listening.

This means that you'd listen not only to the words people say, but to what those words mean. You learn to read between the lines, and understand that listening to people means you'd listen so that you could understand, obtain information, learn, and enjoy—all at the same time. Here's how you can do it:

Pay attention. Look at whoever's talking directly.

Show that you're listening.

Be ready to provide feedback, and to defer judgment for later.

And, make sure to respond appropriately. Do not be biased.

Helping Others Feel Good

Next, you have to realize that a charismatic person is someone who allows others to feel good about themselves, too. If you've ever seen **The Hills**, you'd realize that Whitney Port, although she was not the most popular of the bunch, she still knew how to get people's attention because she thrived on giving compliments. By making others feel good about themselves, they made them see her as a friend, rather than an enemy—and it really worked for her benefit.

You can do the same, too. Instead of being arrogant and always making people feel like they're second best, why not make people feel like they could actually do amazing things, too? See, when you help people feel good about themselves, you make them see you as someone they could trust, and you get to create an environment of positive energy—and these days, that is totally important.

Exercises

In order to help others feel good about themselves, here's what you could do:

First and foremost, be sincere. Do not congratulate people just for the heck of it. Understand why they need to be praised—and start from there. There is nothing worse than an insincere compliment.

Smile, especially while giving compliments. This would make the said compliments real, instead of just making it seem like you're just going through the motions.

Give people sincere praise—and be humble about your achievements. For example, if a person was praised at work today, go ahead and give her more praise—but don't go saying that you can do what she can, too.

Don't be selfish. When asked for help, go ahead and help others out. It will make you feel better about yourself, too.

And, when teaching others, make sure that you are patient enough. Do not act as if you do not have time for them, and make sure that you are willing to help them every step of the way.

Empathy and Emotional Intelligence

And finally, you have to learn how to develop empathy and learn to put yourself in other people's shoes.

According to Psychologists Frank Walter and Heike Bruch of the **Journal of Psychological Behavior**, there is a strong link between charisma and emotional intelligence. Those who are only intelligent by the books are more likely to intimidate people, as opposed to those who use not only their minds, but also their hearts.

You see, by being in tune with your emotions, you also learn to understand what others are going through. You do not become prejudiced or judgmental. Instead, you learn how to see where they're coming from—and you begin to realize that people really have different lives to live. Then, they begin to relate to you, and know that you're someone they could trust—and that's exactly what you'd like to happen!

Exercises

Here are some of the things you could do to make sure that you get to practice empathy—and most of the tips are from Roman Kznaric of Berkely University:

Be curious about the people you meet. Do not see them as plain strangers, but rather as people who are also going through things. Remember that each person you see has a story.

Put yourself in other people's shoes. It is such a cliché, but it works. Once you learn to put yourself in other people's shoes, you also begin to see how their mind works. When people around you make certain decisions that make you raise your eyebrows, understand where they are coming from. Remember they are not you. Listen—and also learn how to open up.

Be ambiguous. Learn to see different sides of any given situation. This doesn't mean you're going to side with the bad people, but rather that you'd also learn to see what made them that way—or why things ended up this way.

Chapter 8: Living Our Limbic Legacy

Before diving straight into the practical tips and techniques for successfully developing a high level of emotional intelligence, it's important to take a look at exactly why and how the body exhibits theses behaviors and reacts in the way it does in the first place. Nothing here is entirely cut and dry but if you can understand the base psychological and physiological processes behind E.I. you can much more reliably develop it within yourself.

Nature vs. Nurture

It's typically very difficult to convincingly or definitively settle a nature vs. nurture debate in favor of one over the other when it comes to human psychology and behavior. Knowing exactly how much of our behavior is derived from our genetics, how much we acquire from our parents and ancestors so to speak or through our environmental influences can be a tough causal link to substantiate either way.

However it's certainly an interesting question to pose and the argument with regards to emotional intelligence is no different.

Goleman himself argues that many of the emotional competencies which make up his Mixed Model are not entirely innate within us, but rather can be learned and developed over time to achieve the high levels of E.I. required for optimal performance and success. He however does state that humans are indeed born with some level of E.I. or at least the potential to develop it which is the biggest determining factor when it comes to the emotional competency level they can reach.

Emotional intelligence in humans is undoubtedly part of our evolutionary make-up along with the rest of our anatomical and behavioral traits. It's really just a case of deciphering exactly how much E.I. is genetically inherited and how much is learnt from environmental influences.

The Old Mammalian Brain

However what isn't in doubt is the development and influence of the limbic system on our psychological behaviors when it comes to emotional intelligence influences brought about by human interaction. Basically any thought that originates in the spinal cord must pass through "rational" part of the brain, the frontal cortexes in order to be rationalized, conceptualized and understood.

However before it reaches these structures a thought must pass through limbic system, the more primitive part of the brain where they become "emotionally charged" meaning that we have an emotional reaction to an event before the complex cognitive prefrontal lobe can engage and make sense of it.

"The emotional brain responds to an event more quickly than the thinking brain"

(Daniel Goleman)

The limbic system isn't a single structure within the brain but rather a set of structures which are located on both sides of the thalamus and positioned just below the cerebrum. It is sometimes referred to as the paleomammalian cortex or the "old mammalian brain" owing to the time period in which it evolved within us.

Essentially these were the first structures that set us apart from our reptilian ancestors, an addition and upgrade of hardware to the primitive structures of the archipallium which is comprised of the brain stem, medulla, cerebellum and oldest basal nuclei. These structures are primarily concerned with just the base sensory organs and simple motor functions, the starting point of any complex organism.

But the limbic system can do much more than this, as a system it supports a host of other functions including emotional regulation, long-term memory capability, ambition and all types of motivational behavior in general. It is basically the driving seat of our emotion center, as the structures heavily influence the endocrine system which intern regulates the dopermaneric pleasure responses to natural and recreational 'highs' alike.

The limbic system also has heavy input on the autonomic nervous system which mediates the 'fight or flight' response within us which can have many knock-on effects to our emotional state as well. However all of these elements are still very base and primitive components with regards the human biological make-up but which still affect our day-to-day lives in a big way even today.

As much as we try to escape this ancestral legacy with the development of the outer neocortexes which provides the machinery that primes us for complex decision making cognition, we are constantly held back by an undersized prefrontal lobe and over powering limbic system. Don't get me wrong, I would certainly rather live in a world that allowed for the emotions of love, connection and compassion which the limbic system affords, but the flip side of this is fear, jealously and aggression which is elicited from these primal centers in exactly the same way.

Now you might be wondering what exactly this has to do with emotional intelligence and the answer is in a monumental way. Essentially what you are doing when you are attempting to develop E.I. is foster the positive parts of this limbic system activity i.e. bonding, rapport building and compassion whilst downplaying the negative side such as fear, anxiety and anger.

Emotional intelligence also comes heavily into play when trying to read someone to develop the social awareness aspects of E.I. which are crucial. What you are actually attempting to do is read the emotional cues the other person is giving away. The physiological changes the body produces naturally, unconsciously and automatically which is almost impossible to mask. This may include getting flush in the face when embarrassed or perspiring when nervous. Trying to control the volume and tonality of the voice when angry or fidgety movements of the body when anxious, it's very difficult to do.

These physiological responses were once highly useful as they were the only means for us to communicate what we were thinking or feeling. They are still very relevant even in today's world of modern speech with regards to conveying emotion, and this can certainly work in your favor when developing the social E.I. you are looking for.

Essentially emotional intelligence requires very effective symbiosis and communication between the newer wet wear of the rational brain with older more primitive emotional structures of the limbic system. There is a term for this communicative ability and brain development in general which neuroscientists refer to a "neuroplasticity". It's basically the process of forming new neural pathways and connections in the brain in response to new learning.

Using certain strategies to develop your own E.Q. levels is no different. When performing these learning techniques you are strengthening the billions of microscopic neuron pathways lining the road between the old emotional centers and the newer rational structures. This also allows for these pathways to branch out, much like a tree to form new connections with surrounding cells again improving overall capacity and cognitive ability. It has been estimated that a single cell can grow up to 15,000 new connections with its surrounding neighbors.

This process essentially further increases the rate of the positive feedback loops and ensures that like anything else that is practiced consistently and over time, it becomes habitual in nature and easier to perform in the future. Emotional intelligence is therefore a skill which is learned like any other.

Chapter 9: 15 Brilliant Tips And Tricks For Reading People

Now that you've gained some expertise about analyzing people' behavior, let's sweeten the deal and give you even more amazing tips and tricks to read people like books.

Here are 12 amazing strategies that will give you insights into what people are thinking and feeling to help you understand them better, and develop even stronger interpersonal relationships.

Even seemingly innocuous questions such as "How are you today?" may be an attempt to establish your baseline, thus setting the stage for further probing and inquiries. This technique is typically used by salesman and business associates. If you're trying to establish someone's baseline, gently probe them about how their day was or how they are doing today. It opens the gates for further discussion, probing and negotiation.

Ask more open ended questions if you want to set an initial baseline for interpreting people.

Former FBI agent Joe Navarro offered many effective tips on reading people in Psychology Today, one of which included avoid vague questions after establishing a baseline. A rambling individual is tough to interpret. Therefore, ask straightforward questions that have a direct answer, which makes it easier for the questioner to detect deception. Don't look or appear too intrusive. Simply throw a question and observe minus interruption.

Clues that convey discomfort, stress, and distress include a furrowing brow, clenching jaws, compression of lips and tightening of facial muscles. Similarly, if someone is shutting their eyes for longer than a regular blink or clearing their throat, there's a high chance they're stalling. Leaning away from you or rubbing hands against their thighs or head is also a sign of high stress.

Children are brilliant subjects to practice on when it comes to detecting liars. If you're looking for signs to spot a liar, simply observe what children do when they lie. Annie Duke, a renowned professional poker player, and cognitive psychology doctoral student suggested that kids are an excellent source to pick up cues about deception.

Adults pick up deception skills to bolster social interactions and personal relationships, which kids haven't mastered at that stage. Therefore, they are pathetic at lying. Every sign is clearly visible because they aren't yet adept at the art of lying. Therefore, observing clear signs of deception in them gives you the ability to spot the same signs in adults.

This, of course, comes with its own fine print. Some people will be better at lying than others. Those who have mastered the art of deception will obviously be well versed in hiding signs of untruth.

When someone nods excessively in an exaggerated manner, it means he is simply conveying his anxiety about your opinion of him. The person is also likely to think that you aren't confident about their abilities.

Our brains are by default hardwired to interpret power or authority with the volume of space occupied by someone. For instance, an erect posture with straightened shoulders conveys authority. It communicates that you are occupying the optimum available space.

On the other hand, slouching is occupying less space and presenting yourself in a more collapsing form, thus demonstrating reduced power. People who maintain a good posture automatically command respect on a subconscious level.

Genuine smiles are easy to tell apart from contrived or exaggerated smiles. When a person is genuinely delighted to see you or by the conversation they're having with you, their smile reaches the eye. It also slightly crinkles one's skin to form crow feet. Smile is the single largest arsenal people use to hide their true feelings and thoughts.

If you want to tell whether a person is smiling genuinely, watch out for crinkles near the eye corners or crow's feet on the skin. The smile is most likely a deception in the absence of these signs.

Did you know that a genuine smile is called a Duchenne smile? It is believed that a smile can never be faked, however hard a person tries. Have you ever wondered why you or someone ends up looking so awkward in pictures? It may appear on the face of it that we're smiling, but we're actually only pretending to smile. Since a genuine smile elevates your cheeks a bit, there are bound to be some crow's feet, which bundles up just below the eyes. Body language experts say this is tough to fake.

You actually need to experience a happy or joyful emotion to be able to create that expression. When you're not comfortable from within or not experiencing genuinely happy emotions, the expressions just do not fall into place.

Look out for micro expressions. If you observe people closely, you'll notice that their real thoughts or feelings (and not what they're trying to convey deceptively) will be flashed on their face in the form of micro expressions.

Sometimes, while trying to come across as consoling, they'll quickly let off a smirk that can last 1/15th of a second. This is because their thoughts and expressions are syncing involuntarily for a moment.

Next time you're traveling by aircraft, notice how flight attendants smile with the help of their mouth but their eyes are blank, and the eyebrows are in a positioned in a scowl when you ask for more drink.

The truth almost always slips out in the form of these tiny expressions or micro expressions. While it isn't difficult to fake body language, look out for the not so subliminal cues, which are a clear giveaway. It's pretty much like shooting stars; you've got to see it fast before it disappears.

Avoid making assumptions. One of the best tips you can receive while analyzing people is not to make prior assumptions or have any sort of biases or prejudices. Sometimes we get to analyze people with a clear prejudice and think we've already found what we've been seeking. For example, if you assume (based on prejudices etc.) that a person is angry, then all their actions and words will seem like there's a deeply hidden anger within them. You will find only what you are looking for.

For instance, if we go to a person's workplace assuming that he is totally disinterested in the job or dislikes it, we'll assume his concentration or lack of cheery approach as absolute disinterest in the job. He may be strictly trying to focus on his job as opposed to hating it. Not everyone grins and laughs when they are enjoying their work. Sometimes, they are just involved in performing it more diligently.

Another important point is to avoid judging others people's personalities based on your own. For instance, in the above scenario, if you truly love your job, you'd have a more positive, grinning and happy expression as opposed to a more somber look. However, not everyone shares your unique traits, behavior, attitude, beliefs, and values.

Identify behavior patterns. Take for instance you're flying in an aircraft, and a particular cabin crew member looks really pissed off while talking to a passenger seated near you. Now, you can quickly jump to the conclusion that he/she has an inherently arrogant, impatient and hostile personality.

However, he/she may have just fought with his/her partner before boarding the aircraft, and may still be carrying the anger within him/her. You really can't tell if it's the former or later until you observe a clear or repetitive pattern.

Does she look particularly annoyed when passengers ask for something? Well, then you've spotted a pattern. If not, you're just being plain unfair in judging him/her based on a single isolated pattern that originated due to another external situation (argument with her partner)

Looking for patterns helps you analyze people more objectively and accurately.

Compare behavior. When you've noticed that someone is behaving particularly out of sync with a group of people or in a specific setting, observe whether they display the same behavior in other groups too. Also, if someone is acting slightly off the normal course with a person, try and gauge if they repeat the same actions with others too.

Continue to observe the person's actions in multiple settings to gain a comprehensive insight of his personality or behavior. Does the individual's expression or gestures change? Does his posture undergo a transformation? What about the voice and intonation? These clues help you know if the behavior you observed initially is a norm with them or simply an exception.

Notice people's walk. The way a person walks can reveal a lot about him. People who are constantly shuffling along demonstrate a clear lack of coherence of flow in things they take up.

Similarly, people walking with their head bowed reveals a lack of self-confidence or self-esteem. If you do observe one of your employees walking with their head down, you may want to help build the person's spirit. Appreciate him more in public and give him tasks that demonstrate your faith in him. Approach him by asking him open-ended questions during meetings to get him to talk more and bounce ideas off people.

Power play with voice. Much as people like to believe, the most powerful or commanding person is not the one at the helm of the table. It is the person with a confident, firm and strong voice. Confidence denotes power.

At any conference table or business lunch, the most powerful and influential/persuasive individual is the one who has a confident and commanding voice, and a huge smile (smiling is a sign of effortless confidence almost like the person is so good, he doesn't have to try too hard).

However, do not confuse a loud voice with a confident/strong voice. Merely speaking loudly won't earn you respect if you sound shaky and confused.

When you're pitching an idea/product to a group of decision makers or people in general, watch out for people with the strongest and firmest voice. These are the people the leader may generally rely on for making decisions or these are the group influencers. When you learn to observe and identify the strong voices, your chances of a positive outcome increase drastically.

People in power often keep their voice low, relaxed and maximum pitch. They don't speak in a tone that elevates in the end as if they are asking a question or sounding uncertain/doubtful about something or looking for approval. They will spell their opinion in a more statement like manner by employing a more authoritative tone that elevates in the middle of a sentence, only to drop down in the end.

Stand opposite a mirror to observe your own body language. Give yourself various scenarios (party, informal outing with friends, a business presentation) and start talking like you would in these settings.

Being aware and conscious of your own body language in varied settings will help you identify patterns of other's body language too. Not just the mirror, the next time you find yourself at a negation table or first date, try to be more aware of your body language and the impression you are trying to convey. This will help you decipher the other person's thoughts and emotions more effectively through their body language.

Observe your own body language without being self-conscious or judgmental. Look how your eyes light up when you are talking about someone you care for deeply, notice how your eyebrows crink when you are speaking to someone you don't really like or trust. This will help you gain a better understanding of other people's thoughts and feelings.

Notice everything from your eye movements to gestures to posture. This will help you to exactly understand what you need to watch out for while analyzing other people.

By tuning into your own underlying feelings and emotions, you will be able to judge other people's body language, words and actions more accurately.

When people try to manage their body language by misleading others, they concentrate on their postures, facial expressions, gestures, and postures. Since their legs movements are more unrehearsed, this is where you're most likely to find deception. When in stress and duress, they will display signs of nervousness, fear, and anxiety with their legs.

If you watch closely, their feet will fidget, shift and wrap around each other make increased movements. The feet will involuntarily stretch, kick and curl their feet to eliminate tension.

Research has revealed that people readers will enjoy higher success analyzing a person's emotional state just by observing his/her body. Even though you may not be aware of it until now, you've been intuitively responding to leg and foot gestures all the while.

Chapter 10: Signs Of Low / High

Emotional Intelligence

No one teaches us about emotional intelligence. We started going to school as toddlers and keep on doing it until we are fully grown, and yet, there is not a program that shows how to manage our feelings and how to have better relationships. Moreover, our culture is full of emotionally negative behaviors accepted as common. Slaves of our feelings. Daniel Goleman, popular author of EI books, tells you there are three ways how people deal with their feelings: you can be aware of them, trapped by them or resigned about them. Whenever we think we have certain feelings, and we can't do anything about them, we lack EI; it doesn't matter whether we only feel defeated by them or if we have accepted we have them and try to move on. The right way to live with our feelings is to be aware of them, handle them and let them happen naturally. Misery loves company. Unfortunately, we tend to use our personal relationships as fertile land for our seed of misery. Think about it, when people feel sad, the usual reaction is calling a friend and talk about it, right? What happens when it has been six months, and they are still calling friends to do the same? What happens when sadness, anger or pessimism become our reason to get up in the morning? People with high EI are simply not obsessed with negative feelings; they are not even obsessed with the positive ones. EI assumes that when we are emotionally healthy, we are interested in life and its positive features instead of living drowned by every negative thing that happens. Losing grip. Someone with high EI will never lose one's nerve. People who usually are nice and polite, and one day get grumpy about everything, are operating under the same pattern as people who wake up one day and start shooting others. Losing one's nerve is a very common sign of low EI. Why? Because it usually happens when we are so full of frustration and anger that we explode. And it is obvious that someone who doesn't let feelings take the lead will never explode.

Hating your boss. It is totally normal you don't become best friends with your boss; it is also normal to disagree with him or her about a lot of things. What is not normal is to hate people. We have been taught that it is a common practice talking behind people's backs and gossip, even telling lies, however, no matter how normal this is for us. It's not emotionally healthy. When we hate someone, we are only proving our own feelings of insufficiency, and, what is worst, this is not necessarily true. While we can feel inadequate, we may still have the required features for not being it. EI tells us we may not know ourselves very well, so we may have wrong conceptions about who we are.

Lack of respect to you and others. If you are always late, you make promises you don't keep and your image doesn't include being trustworthy, then you have a great opportunity to enhance your life with EI. If you disrespect yourself or others, you need to work on valuing your personal resources in order to respect the people involved with you. Emotional stability enables you to make meaningful progress in valuing what every person deserves. Destructive relationships. If you have always experienced love as something painful, there are very important things you need to learn from EI. While love has different ways to be expressed, any of them includes hurting and crying. This is one of the most important points where culture and emotional health are opposite forces. We are surrounded by hundreds of romantic comedies, books and stories that lead us to believe love has to go through all possible tests to be true. However, in the process of creating nutritious and healthy relationships, pain and hard times are not the right ingredients. Emotional intelligence will help you to know what is good and what is not about your way to bond with others. Living in the past or the future. We are taught to plan our future, we usually hear people talking about how the past was amazing, and there will never be a more glorious time and maybe in their mind that's the way it is. However, if you keep dreaming about an unfeasible future or moaning about a moment that is already gone, then you need to improve that area of your emotional intelligence that will allow you to live the present moment and that way create a better future. Problems to make decisions. A clear sign that you need to learn more about emotional intelligence is how hard it is for you to make decisions. Do you struggle for months to make a simple yet critical change in your life? Do you make fast decisions without having enough information and then you regret the results?

Social Isolation. Regardless of your personal interests, favorite colors, relationship status, etc., you are meant to be a social person. You were created to spend time and build bonds with others. If you prefer spending time with your computer because people are "treacherous" or "boring", there is a lot you can do with your emotional health. You don't need to be Mr. Brightside and become friends with everyone around you, you just need to start thinking like a person and stop thinking like an island.

Chapter 11: The Four Building Blocks Of Eq

The four building
 blocks of emotional intelligence helps us to be aligned to our emotions and to manage others'. They are:
1. Self-awareness
2. Self-management
3. Social-awareness
4. Relationship management
The first two deal with our own emotions and the last two about others'. Let us now look at each building block of emotional intelligence separately.
1. Self-Awareness
Knowing how we feel is the first step to managing our emotions. Self-awareness makes us align with the truth of our personality. It tells you exactly what you are good at and what you are not. For your child, it will translate into maturity, better expressing of his emotions, and better learning. To develop self-awareness in

children, you must teach them to think about what they did, tell them to make decisions on their own, and teach them to reflect on things.

Encourage them to judge their reactions as appropriate and inappropriate. For example, if your child refuses to eat at lunch, instead of having an argument about it, try asking him why he does not want to eat. After he gives you his reason, explain to him your point of view and tell him how you feel. Tell him that you are feeling frustrating because you spent time preparing a meal for them. By sharing your own feelings and emotions with your child and asking them for theirs, you will raise their sense of self-awareness and emotional intelligence.

Helping your child to understand their feelings will help him to manage his moods. He will also get better at recognizing the causes of bad moods and bad behavior. You are teaching him empathy by that he acknowledges others' feelings as well.

2. Self-Management

Self-management must be introduced to children with simple things. For 3 year olds and older children, self-management can start with keeping their toys in place, putting their clothes in the cupboard, and arranging their books. If you set up certain tasks for them to do during a day, it will help them to remember things that they need to do and to do them on time. For example, brushing teeth, having a bath, watching television must be done at certain times. This will teach them self-management at the physical level. Through it, children will learn discipline and organization.

Emotionally, self-management of emotions can be introduced by showing a child alternative ways to behave. For example, if your child comes back crying to you because a child mistreated him, you can give him choices of how he could have responded to the situation.

1. He could have told the child to stop misbehaving.

2. He could have told an adult (the child's mom or guardian) that the child was misbehaving.

3. He could left playing with that child at the first instance of misbehavior.

He always had the option of coming to you with a complain, so do not give him that choice. However, tell him that you are there to support him, but let him discover how he could have handled the situation on his own.

This technique of letting children think of alternative ways of responding can be used to develop self-management in kids of any age. With older kids, you may tell them to consider the pros and cons of every choice so that they make the right decision in the end.

3. Social-Awareness

The first interaction of children is through adults. They learn how they must act in front of others by seeing how you act in front to them. As they begin to play with other children, they discover how to manage their emotions and behavior better. When they start to go to school, they create their own independent social life apart from their parents.

To develop social awareness, you need to allow them to spend time with others alone, and then guide them on how they must respond to different situations. For example, if another child tells your child to do their homework, and your child did it because he could not say 'no', tell him that it is bad to ask somebody else to do your homework. Tell him that he should have told that child to do his homework himself because otherwise that child won't learn. Teach your child to say 'no', but give him a good reason for saying 'no'. This will teach your child to be kind to others while not getting exploited by them.

4. Relationship Management

Relationships are one of the most important factors for our happiness. If we have nobody who loves us and cares for us, no matter how much riches we have, we can never be happy. Therefore, teaching our children the importance of relationships and giving them the ability to manage relationships is essential to ensure they develop good relationships as adults.

Relationship management involves getting the best outcome from a situation. To get there, you need to understand the other person and see how you must respond. An easy way to choose a response is to see its effect. Does the other person respond to -

Care (You will have lots of fun doing it!)

Politeness (Could you please try it? Thank you in advance.)

Firmness (You must do it along with the other kids.)

Threat (If you don't do it, you will not go to play tomorrow.)

Depending upon the personality of the other person, a particular category of response will work on them. Your child will slowly learn this on his own, but if he is having trouble managing relationships, you may observe his responses and then guide him to try a different response and see its results. Only with one or two tries, he should be able to build rapport with the other kids.

Teaching your child to be emotionally intelligent is hugely important for their future happiness and success in life. The more developed their sense of EQ is, the more they will get on well with their friends, family and other people in their lives. They will be able to cope better with difficulties and challenges that they face. They will be able to handle and recognize negative feelings and turn them into positive ones. They will be able to manage emotions such as sadness, anger, fright or angst without letting them take over and become out of control. The more we focus on developing their EQ the better it is for not only them but us too, as we will be inadvertently improving our own emotional intelligence as well.

Chapter 12: Skills You Should Have

The benefits that you gain from emotional intelligence also happen to be the four primary skills that you need to be aware of when you are building emotional intelligence skills. Self-awareness, emotional regulation, empathy, and social skills are all things you want to pay attention to when you are building emotional intelligence.

Because we have already learned about these as benefits, we are not going to go into great detail as to what they are or why they benefit you. We will, however, look at ways that you can begin building these skills so that you benefit from greater emotional intelligence in your own life. Understanding this now will help you discover how you can use the techniques in Chapter 5 to truly build your emotional intelligence.

Self-Awareness

In order to truly be emotionally intelligent, one requires the skill of being self-aware. Self-awareness in emotional intelligence means that you are so in tune with yourself that you have a deep sense of understanding who you are and how you live. With emotions specifically, you know what your emotions are like, what triggers various emotions, and how you feel each emotion. You know when you are feeling these emotions what you are inclined to do if you are not capable of emotional regulation. For example, if you are angry, you would know that you have a tendency to shout and scream, or say things you don't mean. Or alternatively, you may know that you are the type of person who gives people the silent treatment and passive aggressively tears into them for how they have treated you or made you feel.

Being self-aware in the way of emotional intelligence goes much deeper than just your emotional self. The more you know yourself on an intimate and intuitive level, the more control you will have over yourself. In order to proceed with other important parts of emotional intelligence, such as emotional regulation, you have to know yourself deeply.

Imagine a friend or family member whom you are very close to. You can likely determine what will upset this person well before the event ever takes place. Perhaps you want to share news with them that you know they will not be pleased about, for example. Because you know them so well, you also know how you can share the information so that it lightens the blow and is less likely to cause as much upset. You are clearly aware of how you can avoid an argument and share the information without causing disruption and anger between the two of you.

This is the result of you knowing your friend or family member incredibly well. You want to know yourself on this same level. You should know exactly what things make you feel, act, think, or do various things. Understanding your natural reactions and responses to life itself means that you know yourself so deeply that you are aware of who you are and how you are. This is a valuable tool in may ways, but especially with emotional intelligence. When you are this self-aware you are then capable of practicing emotional regulation which is another major skill when it comes to emotional intelligence.

Emotional Regulation

When people think of emotional intelligence,they are often thinking of emotional regulation. This is someone's ability to regulate their emotions in such a way that they can control how their emotions are expressed, when they are expressed, and how much information other people gain as a result. For example, if you lack emotional regulation abilities you are likely to say exactly what is on your mind when you are in the raw state of emotion. Since you are incapable of emotional regulation,you will often say things you didn't intend to say. You may give off the impression that you are depressed, desperate, hateful, or otherwise feeling far more extremely toward a person than you actually are. This is because when we perceive that we are under emotional attack, our first reaction is to attack back. Someone who has not yet developed self-awareness, or who has not yet worked on going beyond self-awareness, will not have these types of emotional regulation skills yet. However, they can be built.

People who are able to emotionally regulate themselves are in a position where they can control themselves in virtually every situation. There is a saying that goes "the only words you can control are those you leave unspoken." This means that you are the only one who determines whether you are going to say those words or not. You have the power to share the knowledge or not. In some circumstances the knowledge may be important to share, such as letting a family member know that a different family member is ill. Others, however, may not be ideal to share. For example, if you don't particularly like a certain family member, it may be better to keep that knowledge to yourself and remain civil and polite so that you are able to enjoy family dinners together without causing disruptions for the occasion.

Another example of when emotional regulation comes in handy is when you are feeling extreme outrage, such as through anger. If you were particularly angry at a customer, for example, for blaming you for something that wasn't your fault, emotional regulation would come in handy. Instead of shouting at the customer or otherwise being rude to them and getting in trouble with your boss, you would have the sense to hold your anger to yourself. Instead, you would be polite to the customer and explain the situation calmly and from your point of view. Then, you would be able to rectify the problem and later work through your own angry emotions in a way that is productive and does not result in you hurting anyone or risking your job.

Emotional regulation is the biggest and most recognizable part of emotional intelligence because the mastery of emotional regulation is typically the biggest sign that you actually **have** emotional intelligence.

Those who are not emotionally intelligent tend to feel emotions deeply and struggle to censor their emotions. They cry, scream, yell, throw anger around, and otherwise misbehave in public because they struggle to manage their emotions. These reactions are often proof that they are incapable of managing their emotions, either due to a lack of understanding of how or a lack of desire to do so. Those who are emotionally intelligent, however, know how to keep their emotions to themselves and express them in more socially acceptable ways that both solve problems and help them to eliminate the emotions effectively.

Many people who are learning about emotional intelligence often confuse emotional regulation with bottling up emotions. The two are very different, although they may sound the same. Because you often hold your emotions in until you can express them appropriately, with emotional regulation many people think that you are not releasing your emotions at all. This is untrue. In fact, when you use emotional regulation, you are actually **more** efficient at releasing emotions because you do not hold anything in. Instead, you are intelligent enough to share your issues and solve problems maturely and later sort through your emotions completely. You do not hold anything in, nor do you say anything you may later regret, thus causing a deeper set of emotional problems. Instead, you are very clear and efficient about dealing with problems as they arise and sorting through emotions accordingly. In the end you are not left with residual emotions or feelings that you did not put forth enough effort to be heard and understood in any particular situation. You know that your point was made, and then you released your emotions attached to the point so that you are no longer hurt or in pain by the situation itself. So, contrary to popular belief, emotional regulation is the complete opposite of bottling up emotions.

Empathy

A combination of self-awareness and emotional regulation lends itself to the skill of empathy, but it won't create empathy on its own. Instead, you must learn empathy in addition to being shown it through the aforementioned skills.

Empathy shows emotional intelligence by proving that you can see all aspects of a situation. When you can see from this perspective it means that you have mastered your emotional regulation process enough that you can actually remove yourself from the situation and see it from all aspects. Being able to see it in this way gives you an idea as to how other people are feeling and allows you to completely or almost completely understand them. Because of this you are then able to develop empathy for them.

While having empathy for others does not mean that you need to feel the same way or change your position on a subject to suit them, it does mean that you can gain a newfound respect for them and discover solutions that are effective for everyone involved.

Empathy is something that many emotionally unintelligent people lack because they simply cannot bring themselves to see from different points of view. Instead, they become so emotionally involved in a situation that they can only see their own perspective. As a result, they are incapable of understanding anyone else. Instead, they see other perspectives as juvenile, ignorant, or otherwise implausible. They are often rude and harsh in how they express their disbelief and opposition, trying to make the other person feel ignorant and small rather than trying to help them see alternative perspectives as well.

People who lack empathy do not try and help everyone see the situation on a grand level and work together to solve the problem. Instead, they fight for one angle and will remain entirely unhappy unless all of the other individuals involved cave and follow that single person's beliefs. If they don't and thosebeliefs are not respected, upheld, or otherwise implemented, they will begin to get aggressive to try and change people's minds. They will clearly oppose the results and will often act out of rebellion and protest to try and get their way.

For example, imagine there are three people on night shift in a stocking position trying to determine how to best stock the store before it opens in the morning. The person who lacks empathy wants the job done as fast as possible and is willing to do it in an unsafe manner to achieve this goal. The other two, however, are not willing to risk their safety and want to do it slower to ensure that everyone is protected. Because one of these two people is the shift supervisor and he is responsible for everyone's safety, he confirms that they are doing it the safe and slow way. Instead of respecting the supervisors wishes and understanding that he does not want to risk their safety or his job, the non-intelligent worker starts to protest. Although he is doing it in the way that is intended to be safer, he is not paying attention close enough for it to actually be safe. Instead, he is moving quickly, throwing things around, and loudly complaining about how "wimpy" the other two are compared to him.

Instead of being polite or respecting his supervisor, he asks to go on a break and is gone for twice as long as his break allows, trying to spitefully pressure everyone into changing their mind and doing it the faster way. Because he does not know how to use empathy, he is being impolite and risking everyone's safety due to his own feelings of frustration.

Social Skills

Being emotionally intelligent means that you carry a variety of social skills. Most of these are a direct result of emotional regulation, self-awareness, and empathy. However, they are very important and should each be regarded as a skill on their own. The more emotionally intelligent you are, the more social skills you are going to have. The less emotionally intelligent you are, however, the fewer social skills you will have. The following is a list of social skills that emotionally intelligent people have:

The ability to persuade and influence people

Effective communication skills

Conflict management and resolution skills

The ability to build relationships and rapport with individuals

Team-working skills; the ability to collaborate and cooperate with others

Change management skills

Leadership skills

Each of these skills is an important social skill that can help you in many situations. Knowing how to use these skills effectively means that you can have a powerful influence on others, as well as on your own life. You can easily move people to see things from different perspectives, encourage people to work well together, and effortlessly resolve conflicts between yourself and others or between others such as people on your team. Because you can build relationships with other people so efficiently, they are more likely to trust you and follow your lead. This means that you have a strong ability to lead others and influence them to make certain decisions.

These social skills have a profound impact on your personal life as well as on your professional life. Through the use of these skills you can have stronger interpersonal relationships with those in your personal life and those in your place of employment. Not only will you develop greater and closer relationships with those in your own life, but you will also increase your ability to have deeper and more meaningful relationships. Similarly, you can also create stronger bonds between yourself and those in your place of work, and increase your likelihood of being promoted since you are regarded as a natural leader.

As you can see, these skills are all incredibly important when it comes to having emotional intelligence. They can help you in many ways, particularly related to excelling through life in some way or another. Now that you understand what these skills are and how they pertain to your success, it is time to start seeing how you can build them!

Chapter 13: Know Your Strengths

Many of us are good at pointing out the weaknesses that we have in life. We know that we may have a temper, that we are shy or don't get along with other people that well, or something else. But the tricky part comes when we are asked what our strengths are. It is not uncommon for people to just make up something that sounds good on the spot, but they don't really feel that tied to it.

Learning what your strengths are and using them in your daily life is an important aspect of your emotional intelligence. It helps you to understand what you should be doing and could give you a higher level of satisfaction and happiness in your life than you could ever imagine. Let's take a look at some of the ways that you can learn about your strengths and why this is so important for your emotional intelligence.

What out for the things that excite you

The best way to figure out what your strengths are, no matter what area of your life you are working on, is to watch out for times when you feel excited. When you go about your day to day life, what are some of the things that make you feel happy and excited to get up in the morning? If you aren't able to say these things about going to work, then look at other parts of your life.

Do you enjoy going to do a workout so you can spend some time alone and think at the end of the day? Do you like it when you can go and volunteer and help out others? Do you like writing or spending time with your family or something else? Each of us has strengths that are unique to us, it is up to us to find what these are and spend some time with them each day so we can feel good.

Don't stick with just your job title

Your job title does not have to define who you are. Yes, there are some people who are in a job that they love and that explore all of their talents and strengths, but this is not really something that is true for the vast majority of people. In order to discover what some of your gifts are, you need to take some time to explore the new roles that are out there.

If your company allows it, consider breaking away from your job title and trying out something new. See if you are able to help out on a project in a different department or at least spend some time getting to know the work that other people in your office do. If you start to notice while talking to them that you feel really excited about what you are doing or hearing, it may be that this is one of your strengths.

Your strengths can definitely be something that you enjoy doing. And maybe while you are working on a new project with a different department, your company will notice how good you are at it and will shift your role. You may have been unhappy in the position that you were in before or felt that you were just stuck with no potential, but when you get out of that box and explore the potential that is available in other places, you can get out of that rut and feel better.

Be proud of what you can do

The media has really started to make this one a little hard to work with. We are always bombarded by the media, seeing how this person can do something that is amazing and this other person topped that person. There are always people who are trying to do amazing things and that is great for them, but that doesn't mean that you aren't an amazing person either just because you can't do all of these things.

In a world where we are always seeing amazing things happen all around us, it is frustrating when we see how mediocre our lives seem to be. We don't take into account all the hard work that we do. Yes, the celebrities have time to go all over the world and start a fashion line while having kids, but they also spend a lot of money on nannies and barely see their kids, while you are a great parent who is always there. Yes, there is that kid who started his own business by 21 and is a millionaire, but he probably got all the funding and clients from his parents so he had a way bigger head start. And yet here you are running as one of the managers at your business.

It is easy to get frustrated when we see how far others get and this can make our fuse a little short at times. But when we take a step back and realize all the great things that we can already do, some of which others in your life may wish they could do, you are going to start feeling a little special. You may be a great parent, good at your job, able to do a special hobby or craft, or something else. Each of us has our own unique talents that help us to get so far in life if we would just stop and realize how great those talents are.

It doesn't matter what someone else is able to do so learn how to ignore that. It is more important that you recognize your own worth and all of the talents that you are able to provide to the world. They may not be that amazing compared to some, but they are unique and realizing this can make you feel much better.

Listen to when praise comes your way the most

If you are uncertain about what your strengths as a person are, it is time to start listening to some of that feedback that is sure to be coming your way. Take a moment to listen to what other people are saying to you when you do your daily tasks. Are people impressed by how well you stay calm and collected when the boss gets upset or throws another deadline at you? Are people impressed that you can do some sort of craft or hobby pretty well? Are people praising you when you take the kids out to the store and the place isn't destroyed afterward?

Of course, these are just a few examples of what people may praise you about, but the point is to listen to that praise. It is so easy to say, "I don't have any talents or strengths" but that is untrue no matter who you are. Everyone has some kind of talent and strength is it just a matter of finding out what they are. And if you are still confused at what yours may be, it is time to start listening to those around you.

If others take the time out of their day to praise you for what you can do well, you can be certain that their praise is genuine and you are actually good at it.

Chapter 14: Tips To Improve Your Emotional Intelligence And Achieve Lifelong Success

Let's now understand why we need emotional intelligence to succeed in life. And if it plays such a pivotal role, how can it be improved?

At the point when emotional knowledge was noticed by the masses, and there were considerations and researches done, there was one very unique and shocking revelation made – people with lower IQ tend to have more emotional intelligence, than people with higher IQ. This was mathematically 7:3 and it was quite difficult for intelligent people to digest. They always thought that their sole wellspring of progress was their IQ. Many years of research now indicate emotional insight as the basic component that separates star entertainers from the common men.

Emotional knowledge is a 'feeling' present in each of us, and it is absolutely intangible. It influences how we behave, explore our own social complexities, and settle on individual choices towards accomplishing positive results. Emotional intelligence comprises of four aptitudes that further fall under two basic competencies – personal and social.

Emotional Intelligence Helps in Predicting Your Performance:

What amount of effect does emotional intelligence have on your achievements? The short answer should be 'quite a lot!' It's an intense approach to concentrate on your vitality, follow on direction and gain positive results.

Your emotional insight is the establishments of a large group of important abilities, as it impacts most all that you do in a regular basis. You can definitely be a top entertainer without emotional intelligence, but the chances are less or simply lesser towards prosperity.

Normally, individuals with a high level of emotional insight are more successful. They tend to earn $29,000 more every year, than individuals with a low level of emotional knowledge. The connection between emotional knowledge and personal profit is direct to the point, that each point increment in emotional insight adds $1,300 to a yearly pay. These discoveries remain constant for people in all ventures and spheres of life. There isn't a task or job in which execution and pay aren't closely related to emotional intelligence!

Achievement and joy are what the most of us look forward to in our lifetimes. Sadly, little is instructed and taught in schools on how to make progress past the scholarly measures. Progressively what is expected to prevail in one's life and profession goes past the scholastic accomplishments. For instance, once you pass the required abilities and IQ tests for a given employment, emotional knowledge is observed to be in charge of 80% of your selection.

How to Enhance Emotional Intelligence?

The correspondence between your sentiments and rational approaches are both directed to the brain. It is the pathway for emotional knowledge and it begins in the mind. Your immediate senses enter this path, go to the front of your mind and then let you ponder about your experience. First they go through the limbic framework, where feelings are produced. This lets us have an emotional response to situations before our reasonable personality can lock that in. Emotional insight requires powerful correspondence between our practical and sentimental approaches.

'Plasticity' is what neurologists used to refer to depict the cerebrum's capacity to change. As you find and practice your new emotional knowledge and aptitudes, billions of tiny neurons coating the street between normal and emotional focuses of your mind expand little 'arms', shaping into branches of a tree and then contact alternate cells. One cell can grow 15,000 associations with the fellow cells! This chain response of development helps us know that it'll be easier to detect our feelings and control them from the next time.

When you train the brain continuously, you keep rehearsing new things sincerely, your mind fabricates the pathways expected to make them into propensities. A little while later, you start reacting to your surroundings with emotional feel rather than stressing about your enhanced emotional intelligence. Similarly, your mind strengthens the utilization of new practices, and the associations supporting old and negative practices vanish or you tend to restrain them well.

Tricks and Tips for Enhancing Emotional Intelligence

Emotional Intelligence is significant in the arrangement, advancement, maintenance and improvement of close individual connections. Not at all like IQ, which does not change essentially over a lifetime, our EQ can advance and increment with our yearning to learn and develop.

EI is important and can impact how fruitful we are in our connections and vocations. Whatever phase of life you're at, you can utilize the seven basic strides underneath, to enhance your Emotional Intelligence and build up your mindfulness and compassion.

1. Work on Observing How You Feel

During the time we tend to spend for commitment, start with one responsibility then go onto the next, meet due dates, react to outer requests. A large number of us put some distance away from our feelings. When we do this, we're much more prone to act unknowingly, and we pass up a great opportunity for the significant information that our feelings are trying to tell us!

At whatever point of time, we have an emotional response to something, we're accepting the information about a specific circumstance, individual or occasion. The response we experience may be because of the present circumstances or the circumstance pushes us to remember an excruciating memory.

When we focus on how we're feeling, we figure out how to believe our own emotions, and we get to be much more skilled at managing them. In case you're learning about the practice, attempt the accompanying activity along:

Set a clock for different focuses amid the day.

At the point when the clock goes off, take a couple of full breaths and notice how you're feeling inwardly.

Focus on where that feeling is appearing. It if is as a physical feeling in your body, then what the sensation feels like.

The more you can follow this, the more it will turn out to be your second nature.

2. Notice Your Own Behavior

As I specified before, a key a portion of enhancing our EI is figuring out how to deal with our feelings, which is something we can just do in case we're intentionally mindful of them.

While you're following and practicing your emotional mindfulness, focus on your conduct as well. See how you act when you're encountering your definitive feelings, and how that influences your everyday life. Does it affect your correspondence with others, your efficiency, or your general feeling of prosperity?

When we turn out to be more aware of how we're responding to our feelings, it's anything but difficult to slip into judgment mode and begin joining names to our conduct. Attempt to abstain from doing that right now, as you'll be much more inclined to be straightforward with yourself, in case you're not judging yourself in the meantime.

3. Take Responsibility of Your Feelings and Behavior

This is likely the most difficult stride, and it's likewise the most supportive. Your feelings and conduct originate from you and not any other person. Accordingly, you're the person who's in charge of them.

In the event that you feel hurt in light of something somebody says or does, and you lash out at them, you're in charge of that. They didn't 'make' you lash out, this they don't control your reaction and your response is undoubtedly your duty.

Similarly, your sentiments can give you proper information about your experience and understanding of the other individual, and in addition your own particular needs and inclinations, but still, your emotions aren't someone else's duty. When you begin tolerating this duty, regardless of how you feel and how you carry on, this will positively affect all aspects of your life.

Work on Responding, Rather than Reacting

There's an unpretentious yet vital distinction amongst reacting and responding. Responding is an oblivious procedure where we encounter a emotional trigger, and carry on in an oblivious way that communicates or soothes that feeling. For instance, feeling chafed and snapping at the individual who has quite recently intruded on you.

Reacting is being aware and knowing how you feel, then choosing how you need to carry on with the reaction you are about to depict. For instance, feeling bothered, disclosing to the individual how you feel, why this isn't a decent time to interfere with you, when might be better, etc.

Work on Empathizing with Everybody including Yourself

Empathy is about understanding why somebody feels or carries on absolutely, and also having the capacity to convey that understanding to them. It applies to us and other individuals. If you rehearse this capacity you will enhance your EI.

Begin by practicing with yourself. When you see yourself feeling or carrying on unquestionably, ask 'Why do I believe I'm feeling like this/doing this?' from the start, your reaction may be 'I don't have a clue', however continue focusing on your sentiments and conduct, and you'll begin to see distinctive answers coming through.

Produce and Propose a Positive Environment

While rehearsing the abilities I've specified in this way:

Mindfulness

Self-duty

Empathy

So, set aside a few minutes to notice what is going admirably and where you feel appreciative in your life. Making a constructive domain enhances your personal satisfaction, as well as it can be infectious to individuals around you as well. Here are some more tips which can help to a vast degree in raising emotional intelligence:

1.Removing Negative Emotions

Maybe no part of EQ is more critical than our capacity to adequately deal with our own particular negative feelings, so they don't overpower us and influence our judgment. With a specific end goal to change the way we feel about a circumstance, we should first change the way we consider it.

2.Ability to Keep Calm and Manage Stress

A large portion of us experience some level of worry in life. How we handle unpleasant circumstances can have the effect between being self-assured versus responsive, and balanced versus fatigued. At the point when under stress, the most essential thing to remember is to keep our cool.

3.Ability to Show Assertiveness and Expressing Complex Emotions when Required

There are times in the majority of our lives when it's vital to define our limits suitably, so individuals know where we stand. These can incorporate practicing our entitlement to dissent, of course without being offensive and saying "no" without feeling regretful. It is important for setting our individualistic needs, getting what we paid for and shielding ourselves from pressure and damage.

4.Ability to be Proactive rather than Reactive

The vast majority of us experience outlandish individuals in our lives. We might be 'trapped' with a troublesome individual at work or at home. It's anything but difficult to give that individual a chance to influence us and demolish our day. What are a portion of the keys to remaining proactive in such circumstances? We ought to find that good aspects or simply give up on something that is not helping us go ahead, but actually putting us low.

5.Ability to Fight Back

Life is not generally simple and we all know that. How we pick the way we think, feel about it and act to life's difficulties can frequently have the effect between trust versus losing hope, positive thinking versus disappointment, and triumph versus overcome. With each difficult circumstance we experience, make inquiries, for example, "What is the lesson here?" or "How might I gain from this experience?" or "What is most vital now?" or "On the off chance that I conceive brand new ideas, what are some better replies?" The higher the nature of inquiries we solicit, the better the quality of answers we will get. Ask productive inquiries in the form of learning and needs, and we can pick up the best possible point of view to help us handle the current circumstance.

6. Ability to Express Your Intimate Emotions

The capacity to successfully express and approve delicate, cherishing feelings is basic to keeping up close individual connections. For this situation, "successful" means offering private sentiments to somebody in a suitable relationship, in a way that is sustaining and useful, and having the capacity to react positively when the other individual does likewise.

EI is a Lifetime Process: Always Remember It!

EI isn't something you grow into yourself and then drop. It's a lifetime practice, and it is conceivable to continue making strides. Notwithstanding when you have a feeling that you've aced these means, always continue your practices and you'll receive the rewards of EI forever!

Chapter 15: Giving Your Child An Eq Quiz

Ask your child the questions below to find out what their present emotional intelligence level is. If your child is young and his vocabulary is very limited you will need to explain the meaning of the questions and the answer choices to him in a way that he will understand.

Questions:

1. List five of your friends:

1.

2.

3.

4.

5.

After each of the name, write whether that friend is aggressive, sensitive, or cooperative.

2. When I get upset while playing with other children,

(Tick or mark the correct answer.)

a. I leave them and I come back home

b. I speak to them and let them know what exactly upset me.

c. I shout at them and do not let them play.

d. I talk to an adult like my teacher and complain about that child that is upsetting me.

3. How happy are you with who you are? Would you like to change:

a. Your hair

b. Your height

c. Changes that you are seeing happening with your body (bodily changes, facial hair).

d. None

4. When I make mistakes,

(Tick the right answer)

a. Try and correct my mistake

b. I shout and throw things

c. Think that I am no good

d. Try and hide it from everyone

5. How would you respond to these situations? Would you be comfortable, uncomfortable, or feel like running away.

Please write C for comfortable, U for uncomfortable, and RA for feel like running away, after the question.

a. When you are given a task that is very difficult to do

b. When someone is criticizing you

c. When people are angry

d. When people are crying

6. How often do you fight or have disagreements with others?

a. Never

b. Many times in a month

c. A few times in a month

d. All the time

7. Do you like to talk to new kids of your own age?

a. No

b. Yes

8. How many friends do you have in total at home and school?

a. More than 5

b. Less than 5

c. None

9. I get angry when:

a. Somebody insults or abuses me

b. I do not win

c. Others who do not do what I tell them to do

d. When others isolate me

10. Do you think that you can learn mountain climbing and climb Mount Everest when you grow up?

a. I might

b. Yes

c. No

d. I don't know

Answers

Your child has a high emotional intelligence if he answered the questions as follows:

Q1 Answer: You are the judge!

Q2 Answer: b. Tell them exactly what upset me

Q3 Answer: None

Q4 Answer: c. Try to correct them

Q5 Answer: More than one C's

Q6 Answer: a few times a month

Q7 Answer: a. Yes

Q8 Answer: c. More than five

Q9 Answer: d. Somebody insults or abuses me

Q10 Answer: c. Yes

The four building blocks of emotional intelligence help us to align our emotions and to manage others'. They are the following:

1. Self-awareness
2. Self-management
3. Social-awareness
4. Relationship management

1. Self-awareness

Being aware of how we feel is the first step towards managing our emotions. We can align with the truth of our personality when we have self-awareness. It tells you exactly what you are and are not good at. With your child, as they develop and mature, he will become better at expressing his emotions. To help develop self-awareness in children you need to teach them to think of what they did, teach them to make decisions on their own, as well as spend time on reflecting on things. It is a good idea that you encourage the child to judge their actions as appropriate or inappropriate.

2. Self-management

You can introduce self-management with simple things to your child. Self-management with smaller children can start with putting their toys in their proper places. You can set up certain tasks for them to do in a day. This will help your child to remember things and to do things on time.

3. **Social-awareness**

Children have their first interactions through adults. Children learn how to act in front of others by watching how you act towards others. Once they start playing with other children, they begin to learn how to manage their emotions better. When they are attending the school they develop their own independent social life apart from their parents.

4. Relationship Management

One of the most important factors for our happiness is relationships with others. It is important that we teach our children the importance of relationships and giving them the ability to manage relationships, this is essential to help ensure that they will develop good relationships as adults. Getting the best results out of a situation is what relationship management is all about.

Teaching your child to be emotionally intelligent is very important for their future happiness and success in life. The more their EQ is developed, it will ensure that they will get on well with others in life. Not only will we develop our children's EQ but inadvertently we will improve our own emotional intelligence.

Chapter 16: How To Unlock Your

Motivation And Empathy

If you are not motivated to work on becoming emotionally intelligent and build better intimate relationships, you will not be able to achieve these goals. Your motivation is a crucial ingredient that helps you achieve these goals and every other goal you set for yourself.

Here is how you can tap into that.

How to Become Motivated to Achieve a Goal

To pursue and actualize any goal, you need to feel compelled to work on it actively and consistently. Unless you feel stimulated from within, you will not work on it. The same applies to becoming emotionally intelligent and to strengthening certain bonds in your personal and professional life. To unlock your inner motivation, you need a strong reason for doing whatever you choose to do.

If your goal is to increase your EI, think about how doing so will benefit you and the positive changes it will bring into your life. To draw a certain loved one or professional associate closer to you, think of why you want to do it. Write down those reasons and go through them repeatedly until they become subconscious. This unleashes your inner motivation, which in turn multiplies your ability to practice self-regulation and work on improving your social skills to achieve your goals.

In addition, to have a better understanding of the feelings of others, you also need to increase your empathy, because when you know what someone else is experiencing, only then can you actually help the person.

How to Increase Your Empathy Towards Others

To have more empathy, dedicate time to understanding and analyzing the pain of others. Take one relationship at a time and focus hard on understanding that specific person's problems.

If you wish to strengthen your bond with a cousin with whom you spent a major chunk of your childhood, spend more time together and try to understand her problems. See how she experiences life and perceives different situations and to feel her emotions as yours. Try putting yourself in her shoes.

As you gain deeper awareness of what the other person goes through, you understand their situation better and are likely to comfort them more in any way you can, which helps strengthen the existing bond. When you understand how tough life is for your friend, you stop nagging him or making fun of him even when you mean no harm. Instead, you can console him, which strengthens the bond.

These little things unleash and multiply your empathy and help you slowly transform into a thoughtful and compassionate leader.

Chapter 17: Using Emotional Intelligence

In Employment And Relationship

Situations

* Navigating in Employment Situations

For the last generation of employees, many people trained in vocational or community college situations, secured a job out of college or training, worked up through the ranks, became a manager or higher level person, and remained with that employer until a 20-30 year retirement. As they retired, a new 'batch' of employees was hired to create a similar cycle.

Today the thought of being at the same employer for less than 5-10 years is the norm. More graduates believe they have the proper skills to move directly into middle or upper management positions. Retirement ages are being skewed and less 'entry level with advancement' positions exist. These trends are expected to continue as more office work is outsourced to temp agencies and online workers to save money. Many fillable positions are being evaluated by the need to have an actual person solely with the company to provide the services needed.

In recent years job markets have bent and swayed due to a number of economic factors. With a high unemployment rate, employers are able to pick and choose over a wide variety of possible candidates for almost any open position. A new set of college graduates emerge after each semester, making an already cramped job hunting landscape more crowded than ever.

Prospective candidates must look for capabilities which will make them more marketable, and prospective employers are looking for ways to match the best candidate with the proper position. It is more important than ever to employers to avoid loss to job turnover and employee dissatisfaction.

Having a soaring IQ (Intelligence Quotient) will mean a great deal to some employers while a person of more average IQ ratings will often suffice. However having a higher EQ can impact almost any person searching for a job, any person currently holding a job, as well as almost any employer with positions to fill.

Workplace training is not viable in many situations; therefore, EQ savvy employers are often looking for people that are already aware of how high EQ scores, increased interpersonal skills, more motivation for tasks which will increase the likelihood of success.

Gaining a new position creates another set of unique problems which a high EQ rating can assist the new employee. One example would be, controlling nervous tendencies while meeting new staff, coworkers, trainers, and supervisors will help a person appear to be more poised and confident. Once the prospective employee has relaxed the atmosphere of the office group, introduction stress can be minimized for everyone involved.

Having empathy for others as well as sensing the overall 'mood' of the workplace can assists a person with skills needed to work with multiple tasks, locations, and work groups. The following key points are listed to summarize the main concepts for the workplace.

Self-awareness: If a person has a healthy sense of self-awareness, they are better to 'roll with the punches' and are accept and learn from constructive criticism than co-workers who take every point personally and negatively.

Self-regulation: It is not necessary to hold every personal feeling inside while in the workplace, however people with a higher EQ score can express themselves with restraint and skill.

Motivation: Emotionally intelligent people are naturally self-motivated. They are more concerned with their purpose than simply obtaining a certain title. They creatively handle disappointments and seek ways to improve rather than succumbing to pity or regret.

Empathy: Having empathy is perhaps one of the most important skills a person can have because they are genuine in their concern for others. They are not tied to the 'only help those who will help me' windmill. They are not concerned with interoffice gossip and are more likely to have a positive reaction to help counteract any negativity in the workplace.

People skills: People who are emotionally intelligent are more likely to be respectful of others feelings, property, and position. Rather than having the climb the ladder at any cost mentality, they are more concerned with performing well, encouraging others to perform well, and seeking the satisfaction of a job well done.

* Navigating in Relationship Situations Everyone wants to have the perfect romantic relationship but few ever find that perfect person that makes living worthwhile. The science behind Emotional Intelligence allows a person to understand how to create a more 'perfect' relationship starting internally. They are able to recognize that shaping their own outlooks often is more successful than being set to shape another into their view of a perfect romantic partner.

An old saying is that we do not fall in love with a person, we fall in love with the way that person makes **US** feel. Going one step further with Emotional Intelligence training, a person can understand how profound that simple statement is to cultivating strong positive lifelong relationships.

Some relationships get 'stuck' over a long period of time. While the couple may enjoy a peaceful coexistence, they have stopped communicating with each other. While it may seem to be the perfect relationship because there is no verbal conflict, lack of meaningful communication intensifications distance between the partners. Without emotional self-awareness, most conversations become pat and boring. The peaceful agreement may simply be an unwillingness to stir up the water. A person must be emotionally self-aware to realize what they need from a relationship and what to provide for their partner in return.

Discussion styles vary between couples, families, and sometimes economic or social settings. Some couples talk timidly to one another, while others may tend to have shouting matches and zealously disagree. The fear in a strong relationship is not of conflict but how that conflict is resolved. We do not wish to be in a relationship with a parrot that mimics agreement on every point. A relationship without conflict simply cannot exist. But emotional intelligence teaches us to air our differences without humiliation, degradation to the other party or insanely insisting on constantly being in the right. An emotionally strong couple can have open conversations that are respectful to the other. There are points which they may never agree upon. But having self-awareness, empathy for the other person, and self-regulation, they are able to reach an agreement to disagree on certain points. The relationship can move forward positively without either person feeling injured or wronged.

No one person can meet another's needs 24/7 on every level of the relationship. A person who expects too much sacrifice from the other member of the relationship can add unhealthy levels of stress that will typically surface in other connection levels. Having positive friendships and outside interests not only strengthens social networking, and brings new a breath of fresh air to the relationship, but helps keep a spark shining. This is not to say that extra-marital physical or sexual associations fall into this category. If a situation of this type evolves from a positive outside friendship, having the faith to be able to discuss the issue and resolve it before any permanent damage ensue is critical to keeping the relationship intact.

When both people feel comfortable expressing their needs, fears, and desires, trust is strengthened. Nonverbal cues—body language like avoiding eye contact, leaning forward or away during a caress, or touching someone's hand—are often overlooked but are very important. Keeping our lives balanced enough to have empathy for our partner will aid it noticing subtle non-verbal cues. However, knowing when to notice and when to notice without overreacting to every event comes with time and knowing the personalities involved.

Chapter 18: What Is A Team ?

The label is often used along with 'group' and yet a team as we understand it has a very specific connotation. The difference very largely lies in the course of action. A group can exist and yet not very achieve much, a team, on the other hand, is action orientated. It has a clear purpose, direction and which is shared by its members.

There are a number of features of a team which make it unlike a group:

In a proactive team, members share a high-end commitment to achieving a common objective.

Members of an effective team experience a high level of satisfaction from being part of and working within the team.

In an effective team, members work well together in a combined way, with a high level of responsiveness and appreciation of their overall strengths together.

A reactive team shows a high potential for solving its own difficulties. The skills exist and there is a readiness to act, this action is immediate.

Most important from the organization's point of view is that a proactive team is a team creating high quality results. High quality results, it could be reasonably reasoned, is the accomplishment of an effective team.

The qualities of an effective work team are, therefore, identifiable by you as a leader, quite precise and measurable. Although any group can possess any or all these characteristics, an effective team will consistently display them all.

What conditions make a team effective?

Clear Objectives: The team's overall objective needs to be identified and defined by the leader in terms which allow each member to know the same goal. The leader has an important role in conveying a clear idea of what the organization expects from the team. A style which encourages a questioning approach is likely to reveal any members' reservations, misunderstandings or questions which need to be positively addressed.

Appropriate Leadership: Leadership is a cooperative function based on the requirement of the task rather than through consideration of formal role or position-based power. This requires a lot of flexibility in identifying and allowing other team members to exercise real leadership when a member's skills are more appropriate to the team at that time. There is an important leadership function. It is one of using your skills to develop the team and make sure that time is assigned appropriately for team-building activities.

Suitable membership: For a team to be able to work productively, its members must display the range of skills, knowledge and experience and the right combination of these for the project it is tasked to do. All members are valued for what they can give and are encouraged to develop themselves. No time is wasted on considering what members cannot achieve. The emphasis is on the strengths of the individual team members.

Commitment to the team: Team members experience real strength from their membership and the sharing of shared goals. They are willing to invest considerable energy in the interests of the team. Membership is highly valued and member behaviour is strongly influenced by considerations of team success. The leader has the role of binding all these facets together. This is far different from the rather simple view of just being with a group of people who get on well together and enjoy the others' company.

A supportive team climate: The order of the day is participation and personal responsibility. Team leaders can foster this environment from the outset, encouraging and building up the team members. Those members are respected enough to contribute in a mature fashion. Leaders demonstrate that self-control replaces imposed control. Responsibility is widely shared throughout the team on a rational basis, given the attributes and other strengths among all the members. Members are invited to contribute ideas, question the team and its activities openly without fear of censorship, condemnation or reprimand. The only condition is that the members' behaviour is with the best interests of the team and its performance at its very core.

Getting things done: The leader is guiding at all times. The successful team not only knows where it is going, it knows from where it came and when it has arrived. It sets out performance markers and indicators and establishes ways in which the team's movement toward realising the targets can be measured. It is important that performance targets are ones that epitomise something of a challenge to the team and its members without being unattainable and subsequently lower the moral of the whole team. When the right standards are set, the team's energy is pointed towards achieving the end result. Team performance is constantly being appraised by the leader, in order to identify any problem areas in the team's trajectory or issues being experienced by members. This is an important responsibility for the team leader.

Working techniques: The team needs to invest time and effort into formulating working techniques, methods, procedures and rules to project the team toward its goal in the most competent way consistent with preserving those other qualities allied with effective teams. These include techniques for making decisions, solving problems and coping with anything which disrupts and blocks progression to the end result.

Learning: The leader, the team and its members learn from their experiences, including their mistakes. Mistakes made in good faith do not lead to heavy consequences, but are included into expectations about the team and its members mature over time.

Problems are reviewed for what they can contribute to the individual and collective advancement process. Constructive criticism, based on logic and rationality is intended to help the team and its members grow in competence. This is most certainly welcomed as team progression. This places a high price on fact-to-face skills associated with coaching and then giving feedback. They will predominantly be highly valued skills when used effectively by the team leader.

New members: New team members are quickly included into the team, their strengths are identified by the leader, and their contribution is defined. All effort is used to help the new member prove his or her value to the team as quickly as possible.

Managing the group: An effective work team recognizes the importance of monitoring the team itself and the way in which it is working under pressure. Understanding something of 'group dynamics' is an area of knowledge and skills which is highly developed in very effective teams. The leader can encourage this method by example and initiating this with the team. Allocating time and energy to understanding and managing relationships is an important investment. The team leader should be able to display considerable skill in this respect. An obligation for monitoring events is not invested in the team leader alone. It is shared among members, although some will be more suited than others and show preferences in the direction of what is called team maintenance.

Relationships with other teams: An effective team also invests time and energy into developing ground rules for managing its relationships with other teams in a positive and productive way. This includes identifying areas of work where collaboration would clearly help one or both teams achieve results more efficiently or effectively. It includes maintaining open contact and frequently reviewing tasks priorities. Resources are shared where this will help progress toward a broader, but understood and shared, organizational objective. Joint problem solving is widely adopted and the tendency to 'blame others' is replaced in effective team working with a direction of effort toward understanding problems and finding solutions.

Success: The effectiveness of a team grows. All the conditions set out above develop more extensively and readily to the extent that the team meets with early, continued and acknowledged success. The saying "Nothing succeeds like success," is entirely applicable to the development of an effective team and in the process of developing and reinforcing the conditions underpinning demonstrated effectiveness. Two possible problems exist for very successful teams. First, they may be seen as so competent that they attract more work than they are able to handle resulting in overload and decline in performance. They may have to learn to turn down assignments to project themselves onto high end projects that they can grow with. Even if they attract more resources of money and people to handle the extra work, they may suffer from problems of being too big losing the ability to communicate due to size and the quick change to the dynamics of the team if it spread too thinly. Even including internationally and will almost certainly need to restructure into smaller satellites if they are to continue successfully.

The second problem for the successful group is one of being complacent. They can sit down on previous successes. Their very success and cohesion becomes their own worst enemy, and they find it hard to respond to new circumstances and changes. Some groups guard against this by ensuring that they get a fairly regular turnover of people to keep them on their toes.

Chapter 19: Emotional Intelligence,

Feeling Good, And Self Confidence

Self-confidence is really far from being stable. Day after day, it can fluctuate. It easily changes depending on the stimuli that you encounter. Despite this instability, it is considered as a very important component of emotional intelligence. And yes, the best parameter for this is not really published. For as long as you feel good about something and it promotes your self-esteem, it can somehow help you develop your self-confidence and your emotional intelligence.

Having self-confidence is very important because it makes a person a lot stronger in terms of emotions. It can also make him resilient despite the stress that may be experienced on a daily basis. According to research, when a person's self-confidence is low, facing rejection is extra painful. On the other hand, if you are very much confident about yourself, you tend to move on faster despite the rejection.

Motivation level drops when a person has a poor self-confidence. After experiencing failure, a person who lacks confidence might give up easily. On the other hand, a person with a high level of self-confidence is emotionally intelligent because he finds a way to redeem himself, get back up again, and try to find a way to feel good once more.

If you wish to put it in terms of analogy, self-confidence can be regarded as a person's emotional immune system. If a person's self-confidence is high, then a person can consider himself resilient despite the "injuries" brought about by failure, anxiety, rejection, and stress. If you wish to boost your self-confidence, then you have to start preparing your resilience and emotional intelligence and strength as well.

According to research, boosting one's self-confidence has a great impact in a person. In an experiment, several people were studied for their reaction in anticipation of a mild electrical shock that is going to be given to them. Half of the participants were given some pep talk and self-confidence boosters. On the other hand, half of the participants were not given this kind of booster. Those whose self-confidence was boosted felt better than the rest because their anxiety level is relatively low. In the end, participants were told that no amount of electrical shock is going to be administered to them. Only their reactions were studied in the process.

So what exactly can boost a person's self-confidence? Experts say that simple self-affirmations can do a lot in boosting a person's self-confidence. Every time you do a great job, try to tell yourself that you are happy about it.

Note that there are many self-affirmation exercises that you can learn in order to boost your self-confidence. By learning these, you can find yourself better protected from the psychological "injuries" that are encountered every single day.

Chapter 20: Sixth Step To Emotional

Mastery – Compassion

The common mistake of other people who discuss emotional intelligence is that they make it look like it only involves making one's self better. That is not entirely true. Emotions can be fueled by people. It is people who can intensify an emotion and turn it into passion. That is why it is important to always think about other people when dealing with your own emotions.

Most people always regard compassion as simply pity or sympathy over other people's suffering. It is way more than that. Compassion includes the desire to help other people feel better. Compassion requires a concrete action to improve the situation and make other people feel happier.

To become an emotional genius, you should learn that being compassionate does not discriminate. People who are truly compassionate do not feel better about themselves because they see that other people had it worse. They strive to make themselves feel better by making sure that other people do not suffer. There is big difference between helping just for the sake of doing something, and giving one's self in service for another to create a big change.

You do not need to be a saint and look for extremely poor people to become compassionate. You can do it every day. Make others feel better by smiling at them. Lend others a helping hand. Let a fearful friend know that you have his or her back. Little gestures of compassion can make a big difference.

Chapter 21: Lack Of Empathy In Relationships, What To Do?

It is difficult to realize exactly where a lack of empathy comes from , that is to say, from one or both of the partners, since generally everyone has the feeling that they know what their partner needs, that they understand, even if it is not so and it is only a projection about what they believe the other person needs.

It is important that in a loving bond, there is empathy and an emotional connection that causes both parties to feel truly understood and valued. So if you feel that there is a lack of empathy in your partner, do not worry, there are things you can do or that both can do to begin to have a better emotional connection and feel comfortable in the relationship.

Lack of empathy in relationships: why does this happen?

All, or almost all, people have the belief that we are empathic and that we can easily put ourselves in the place of another until some situation occurs that makes us realize how difficult it sometimes is. One of the relationships in which we can appreciate this more is in the couples relationship - lot of couples' crises are caused by a lack of empathy between them.

Empathy is the ability that people have to to see things from the other person's perspective, thereby ceasing to impose our own beliefs and ideas onto a situation. Empathic people can do this very easily and often go into the inner world of the other person in order to really understand the way they may be feeling.

So a lack of empathy implies that for the non-empathic person it is impossible to forget for a moment about themselves and their desires, ideas or beliefs and be aware or understand what the other person is really feeling, especially if that person thinks and lives very differently from them. When this happens at the level of a couple, one or both parties often feel misunderstood and undervalued, and have the feeling that their partner totally forgets them. All this undoubtedly in the long term causes a series of conflicts to be unleashed, and if they are not resolved, they may seem endless.

The lack of empathy in a couple occurs precisely because one or both parties are not accustomed to entering the world of the other person, to recognizing what they need or want. Many times this happens unconsciously, and one or both think that they always put themselves in the place of the other, when they are in actuality putting their own interests first. This doesn't mean that a person is simply good or bad for doing this, rather it is about having or not having the awareness of what is being done and not having practiced it enough.

How to act in the absence of empathy in relationships: 5 tips

Respect your partner's opinion. Each and every person has the right to believe, feel and think in the way they want and that is something we have to respect. Many people try to change another's way of thinking or seeing things and make them think as they do. So it is necessary that you respect the opinions of your partner if you want them to respect your own opinions.

Do not judge your partner. Avoid making value judgments about your partner and labeling him/her. On the contrary, try to put yourself in their place and look at things for a moment from their perspective.

Patience and understanding. It is easy to tell the other person what they should or should not do in the face of difficulties, however, it is necessary to understand that each person is different and what is useful for some may not be for others. For example, if your partner has problems with his siblings because they take advantage of him, instead of telling him that he should not behave like this, get angry with him for his way of acting, etc. The best thing to do is to look at things from your own perspective. In this case, it is probably difficult for your partner to change their attitude, due to the great love they have for their family, because they have always wanted to have a good relationship with their siblings, etc. and apply patience and especially compassion to find a better solution.

Be kind to your partner. Do not forget that education and good treatment is essential to regenerate empathy in a relationship. On many occasions, we forget about things like this that are basic and essential in all kinds of relationships, especially in couples. So it is important that you take care with your words and do not act on impulse to avoid hurting your partner, In short, treat him or her as you would like to be treated.

Try to resolve conflicts in peace. Whenever there is a conflict between the two of you that you know will be a reason for fighting, instead of focusing all your attention on the problem itself, try to see things objectively and focus on finding a solution. Prevent the conflict from getting bigger, tell your partner how you feel and take great care not to assault or hurt their feelings. Focus on how to improve the situation. This will make your partner feel more calm, understood and treated with respect, also over time, you will encourage them to take the same attitude to conflicts arising in future.

Chapter 22: Why Emotions Determine

Your Life

Psychological research has proven that your ability to understand emotions and control them accordingly is integral to your ability to live a successful life. To understand why emotional intelligence is so important, you need to understand the role emotions play in our lives and why having the ability to control them is of such importance.

The first thing to note is that emotions are brain-driven: before the nervous system activates and creates the bodily feelings associated with specific emotions, your mind creates associated thoughts in your mind.

Emotions are important because their role is to evaluate all your circumstances and experiences and from this evaluation, draw conclusions that inform your decisions and actions. From this logic, it is clear to see that most of your decisions and actions are a result of emotional responses, which makes emotional intelligence a valuable ability because the ability to control your emotional responses means the ability to control your decisions and actions.

Although emotions lack sophistication, they make up for it in speed and utility. Speed of particular importance here because once your mind triggers an emotion, the rate at which disordered emotions provide basic, non-cognitive information about a situation is very fast. This means your emotional responses will lack the element of critical thinking and therefore, you are likely to make ill-informed decisions that lead to misinformed actions.

Take the example of a situation that makes you anxious such as the first time talking to a girl you feel romantically attracted to; the anxiety you experience is an emotional response telling you that you are in a new situation that requires further evaluation. As is often the case, since this is a distorted emotional response drawn from being in a new situation, your first decision is to remove yourself from that situation.

On the other hand, when you have a well-developed emotional quotient, instead of giving into the emotional response, which in this case means going with the first non-cognitive decision and removing yourself from that situation, you take a moment to observe the emotion critically and in so doing, determine the best cause of action. In this case, if you really want to approach this girl and make her part of your life, you can recognize the anxiety for what it is, fear that she may reject you, and still choose to act because not talking to her negates your goal of having her in your life.

Emotions are also important because other than what we have discussed thus far, they also serve another important purpose: they inform your mind what to do in different situations, a response that has developed since birth.

Think about it this way.

Our daily lives are full of stimuli and as such, our brains are constantly processing new information because of which, we lack the capacity for reflective processing, and therefore, our brain normally processes this stimuli unconsciously and passively, connecting emotions to actions and then automating them as much as possible.

Take the example of the anxiety reaction mentioned earlier. Because the prospect of a new emotional attachment (and the possibility of rejection) has made you anxious and nervous before, the brain will automatically recognize when you are in a similar situation and trigger similar emotions, feelings, and reactions. This emotional cue system allows you to direct your attention to the actions you intend to take. When emotional intelligence is lacking, you are likely to make an emotion-driven decision but when well developed, you are likely to think the decision through and thereby make sound decisions.

Another important reason why emotions (and emotional control) are of such importance to your overall wellbeing and success in life has to do with the very fact that since they determine your actions, emotions have massive action-driving potential. A great example of this is our different approaches to the completion of a project.

Some of us will experience anxiety until we complete a complete; on the other hand, some will not experience anxiety until the deadline draws near thereby meaning the deadline becomes the cause of anxiety and the driver of action.

The emotionally intelligent have a well-developed sense of how emotions affect their ability make conscious decisions that relate to their motivation and ability to pursue their goals and aims.

As you can see from the above discussions, emotions are very central to your decision-making and action-taking abilities. When you are not in control of your emotions, you are likely to make unsound decisions and take ill-conceived actions. On the other hand, when you have a firmer grasp of your emotions, you can limit emotional reactions, and in so doing, make logic-driven decisions and take well thought-out actions

When used properly, your ability to control your emotional system (and its reactions) can serve as a decision-making advantage. The very essence of emotional intelligence is to teach you how to take a moment to recognize your emotions, think them through, and then capitalize on this emotional response to make decisions and take actions that align with your main aims and goals.

The next chapter continues this conversation and introduces you to emotional intelligence:

Chapter 23: Explaining Emotional

Intelligence

The modern world, with its myriad of screens and ways to make human contact even more fleeting, can make it more difficult than ever to connect with other humans on a personal level. While this is true for everyone, those with a lower level of emotional intelligence (EQ) have an even greater difficulty connecting with others to the detriment of their relationships, personal goals, career and more. While it is not nearly as well publicized as IQ, EQ is just as important as it is what helps to create action out of positive intentions, connect with other people in productive ways and make important life decisions.

EQ is the ability to utilize emotion to identify, understand, use and manage your emotions as effectively as possible to ensure you always communicate clearly, reduce stress, connect empathically to those around you, minimize conflict and maximize success. Your level of EQ also makes it easier to understand what others are feeling and put yourself more successfully in their shoes. This understanding comes from picking up on body language and other nonverbal cues and is essential to getting ahead in the business world and forming long lasting and meaningful relationships.

Those who are perceived as the most successful are rarely the smartest or the strongest, they are the ones who are the best at interacting with others and managing their emotions as well as their responses to stress. IQ can get you in the door, EQ will help you get noticed. EQ trickles down into all facets of life including:

Work performance: The social web of the workplace is difficult to navigate at the best of times, and for those with low EQ it can be extremely fraught with peril. It is important to improve your EQ if you hope to motivate others, excel, and eventually lead your own team. EQ is becoming an increasingly important requirement for moving up the corporate ladder and is something that many companies now require as a prerequisite for advancement.

Physical health: Understanding your emotions means managing them properly and managing emotions are intimately connected to managing stress which can lead to decreased blood pressure, increased risk of stroke, cardiovascular disease and infertility, and, if left untreated, can ultimately suppress the immune system and leave the body open to countless potentially fatal diseases. It can also intensify the effects of the aging process.

Mental Health: Those who let their emotions run wild and do not deal with their stress effectively leave themselves at risk for depression, anxiety and a host of related conditions. What's more, those who cannot find ways to emotionally connect with others run the risk of long term emotional isolation which can lead to feelings of intense loneliness and possibly thoughts of self-harm.

Interpersonal interactions: Those with a firm grasp on their own feelings are more easily able to process their emotions in the moment while at the same time quickly relating to the emotions others are experiencing as well. The increased effectiveness of this type of communication makes it easier to form long lasting and more viable relationships in all types of personal arenas.

Social intelligence: Social intelligence is an offshoot of emotional intelligence that allows for things like separating foes and friends, and also returning the nervous system to a balanced state after times of stress. It is crucial when it comes to determining another person's level of interest, trust, and level of friendliness.

Four pillars of EQ

There are 4 primary attributes that those who have high levels of EQ can be said to embody. They are outlined here and then explained in detail in chapters 4-7.

Self-Aware: Those with a high level of EQ understand the emotions they are feeling as they occur and understand how they may affect their actions. By more clearly understanding their weaknesses, as well as their strengths, they can be more confident overall regardless of the situation.

Self-Control: Those who understand their emotions can control them more easily when required leading to fewer impulsive reactions. They don't just close their feelings off, however, they instead manage them in healthy ways and are also known to take initiative, honor commitments and handle change easily.

Socially Aware: Those with enough EQ are able to easily understand the emotions that others are feeling as well as the roots of those emotions. They can understand emotional tells and cues, are comfortable in social situations and understand power dynamics and their importance in the social structure.

Manage Relationships: Those who understand their emotions also understand how to maintain healthy relationships while still developing new ones. They can influence and inspire others with their clear communication and ability to diffuse conflict. It is for these reasons that they often make good team leaders.

Chapter 24: The Basics Of Emotional

Intelligence

Emotional intelligence is starting to gain as much attention as IQ. For decades, IQ has been the standard for intelligence. Recent breakthrough found that emotional intelligence is just as important as IQ.

The definition of emotional intelligence

Emotional intelligence or EQ refers to the ability to distinguish, utilize, comprehend and cope with emotions in a positive manner. These should help in relieving stress, empathizing with other people, defusing conflict, communicating effectively, and overcoming challenges.

This ability helps in recognizing and understanding the experiences of other people. This helps to form bonds or connections, which is crucial when socializing or dealing with others. The understanding and recognition that EQ provides are basically nonverbal. It is a process that influences one's thoughts and conduct when with others.

EQ is different from intellectual abilities. Intellectual ability is acquired, while EQ is learned. Learning can happen at any stage. Anyone can have the skill set of EQ regardless of age.

History of emotional intelligence

"Emotional intelligence" as a term was first mentioned in 1964, in a paper by Michael Beldoch. It was also used in a paper by B. Leuner in 1966. The first usage was in a doctoral thesis by Wayne Payne in 1985.

The inclusion of emotional intelligence as part of multiple intelligence was made by Howard Gardner in 1983, in his **Frames of Mind: The Theory of Multiple Intelligences.** This came about when Gardner introduced the idea of multiple intelligence. It stemmed from the idea that IQ and other traditional types of intelligences cannot give a full and satisfactory explanation of a person's cognitive ability.

The term "emotional quotient" or EQ was first published in British Mensa magazine, in an article written by Keith Beasley in 1987. Emotional intelligence was described in a model by Stanley Greenspan in 1989. In this same year, EI was further described by John Mayer and Peter Salovey.

Emotional intelligence gained a wider audience when the Goleman book was published. The book was entitled **Emotional Intelligence- Why it can matter more than IQ**. It was published in 1995. It became a best-seller, which contributed to the popularity of the term "emotional intelligence".

The 4 attributes of emotional intelligence

To further define emotional intelligence, know about its 4 attributes. These attributes show what emotional intelligence is and what it includes.

Self awareness

This refers to the recognition of your specific emotions. Self awareness is also about knowing the effects of these emotions on your behavior and thoughts.

Having this attribute indicates that you are conscious or aware of your own weaknesses and strengths. Self awareness helps in developing self-confidence.

There are 2 main parts of an emotion. There is the psychological component and then there is the physical component. The psychological component includes the beliefs, attitudes and thoughts that accompany the emotion. The physical component includes the bodily (physical) sensations that come with the different emotional states.

For instance, when you feel nervous, you have both psychological and physical components in play. In the psychological aspect, you experience thoughts such as doubts and fears. In the physical aspect, you feel "butterflies in the stomach" and restlessness.

Self management

This is the ability to control impulsive behaviors and feelings. It also includes healthy handling of emotions, taking initiative, adapting to changing situations and following through on your commitments.

Self management is about learning better ways to respond to the emotions. Numerous strategies are available to help in positive responses and more effective regulation. Some of the more commonly used effective strategies are:

Channeling into new, constructive ways such as painting and exercising

Staying away from triggers of negative emotions such as environments, people and situations

Reversing negative emotions with new, positive experiences such as listening to motivating movies or music

Doing things that are opposite of the negative emotion

Being a passive observer to negative emotions instead of impulsively acting on it

Empathy

This is about understanding the needs, concerns and emotions of others. You can pick up the emotional cues, recognize the dynamics existing within organizations or groups and being comfortable in social situations.

Relationship management
This entails development and maintenance of good relationships. Communication is clear and working with a team is feasible. Conflict is effectively managed when it arises. Inspiring and influencing others also happen.

The importance of emotional intelligence
Emotional intelligence is important. Most people think that to be successful, one has to be smart. There is a common notion that to be fulfilled, one has to be exceptionally bright. Intellectual capabilities are not the only things that matter. Emotional intelligence is also important.

IQ or intellectual intelligence can help in the journey towards success. Being smart helps to get into college, get degrees or pass exams. But people who are academically brilliant but socially inept will not always be successful. EQ is a huge help in managing the stresses and emotions that come with tasks and challenges.

If you have both good IQ and EQ, you have the vital ingredients to be successful. These factors are most effective if they feed off each other, elevating and building each other.

The effect of emotional intelligence is far-reaching. It has an influence over the following:

Performance

Whether at work or in school, EQ helps in getting through the complexities of socializing. It aids in motivating and leading others. It also helps in achieving excellence in a chosen career.

The influence of EQ in the workplace is becoming more and more widely recognized. A lot of companies today are already considering EQ as just as important as an employee's or applicant's technical abilities.

Physical health

Proper management of emotions also entails proper stress management. If not, then stress becomes a significant factor in the development of serious health issues. Stress is a risk for cancer, obesity, cardiovascular diseases, diabetes, accelerated aging and infertility issues. It lowers immunity and raises blood pressure levels. It also raises blood sugar and puts the hormones out of balance.

Mental health

Stress and emotions allowed to get out of control can directly affect mental health. These increase the risk for depression and anxiety. These will get in the way in forming mutually satisfying bonds and relationships, creating feelings of isolation and loneliness.

Relationships

Understanding and controlling emotions allow for better expression of feelings. It also aids in gaining a better understanding of the feelings of others. This will greatly help towards the formation and development of mutually satisfying, healthy and strong relationships with others. This paves the way for more effective communication. This impact can be seen in relationships at work, in school, community and among friends and family.

The 4 branch models of emotional intelligence
The abilities gained for emotional intelligence can be better understood using the 4 branch models. These models describe the different areas of emotional intelligence and the abilities in each.

Perceiving emotions
This refers to the non-verbal manner for reception and expression of emotions. This stems from the Darwinian idea that emotions developed as a means of communication. One concrete example is the way we perceive facial expressions. When somebody smiles, it is a means of conveying an emotion without using words. This is innate in humans, which is an indication of how emotions play vital roles in communication.

Using emotions
Emotions are used in facilitating thoughts. It enters into the thought processes, guiding and encouraging rational thoughts.

Once emotions influence thought processes, it directs thoughts towards prioritizing things that grabs the attention. Emotions are also important in the creativity process. It influences and drives the expression of creative thinking. For instance, positive moods and mood swings both promote carrying out of creative thoughts.

Understanding emotions

Information can be conveyed through our emotions. For instance, when we are happy, we are conveying excitement and positive feelings to other people. When we are angry, we are conveying the desire to harm or attack another person. Each of our emotions has their own set of possible messages. And with the message comes new set of possible actions.

Our emotions come with a specific set of reactions for every action. Understanding these relationships plays a role in survival.

Managing emotions

We can manage emotions in order to convey the right information and make the action-reaction work for us. It is natural for people to be open to positive emotions and try to block painful, negative ones.

We have developed a comfort one for emotions, where we regulate, promote and manage emotions to further our personal and social goals.

Chapter 25: All About Emotional

Intelligence

The first step to building emotional intelligence is understanding what it really is and this part of the book will therefore ensure you grasp that and also know how applicable it could be in your life. Outstanding leaders and successful people in any field of work distinguish themselves by their ability to recognize their own emotions and those of others and also use emotional informational operatively to guide their behavior and thinking. Emotional intelligence is normally defined as that ability for a person to manage and adjust emotions so that they can adapt to any environment, situation or event.

Emotional intelligence is linked to success because how a person manages their own emotions and also empathizes with the emotions other people display has a huge impact on how effective we are at getting things done with and through people. The thing is that when you work on increasing your emotional intelligence you become better at responding to people and circumstances both at work and home environment. We normally experience our own emotions and those of others every passing moment so learning to manage them is what you need to make a difference in your life.

It is emotional intelligence that allows you to combine thinking with feelings as a way of building good relationships and also making reliable decisions. Emotional intelligence is completely different from cognitive intelligence but still a skill that can be learned. This will be with an aim to change how you view both people and situations. It mostly entails changing the way you work with your emotions and might not be as easy as imagined. Developing emotional intelligence will definitely take you some real time and effort, it being a contributing factor for technical and functional expertise which leads to increased performance.

To confirm your emotional intelligence you should be able to recognize, understand and manage your own emotions and also recognize, understand and influence the emotions of other people. This will be with the knowledge that our very own emotions can actually drive our behavior and impact people either positively or negatively so learning to manage these emotions is for our good and the good of others. The good thing about emotional intelligence is that the more a person understands their reactions under certain conditions, the better they are able to anticipate their behavior and therefore in a position to counter it with a more responsive response.

Why learn about emotional intelligence, you may ask, I always love the idea of being emotionally intelligent because it is what enables one to perform at their best and also connect with people in a more meaningful way. This not only makes you an effective leader but is also a way for anyone to increase their position in any field and also influence success. Any kind of pressure, challenges or obstacles normally changes how our brains function and mostly diminishes our ability to think, make decisions and also connect with others. Emotional intelligence however allows you to manage your emotions under such conditions and you will therefore have no room to maintain limiting thoughts, give up or react negatively in any other way.

Emotional intelligence is believed to be inclusive of three skills, the ability to identify your own emotions and those of others, ability to harness emotions and apply them to problem solving and thinking and lastly the ability to manage emotions. These are factors you can see in specific people in our lives who always know what to say and how to say it in all situations making sure that no one is offended. Such are the kind of people who have a high degree of emotional intelligence and apart from understanding themselves very well are always able to understand other people's emotional needs.

If you are looking to achieve success in every area of your life and also be able to recognize emotions, understand what they say and realize how your emotions affect people around you then that journey should begin by cultivating as much emotional intelligence as possible. Explained below are the main skills of emotional intelligence:

Perceiving emotions: as an emotionally intelligent person you need to have the ability to recognize all your emotions in every life situation and also the emotions of those around you. This way you can know the best way to react towards those same situations. This puts you in a position where you can actually allow yourself to only be guided by the positive emotions and letting go of the negative ones.

Managing emotions: this is another skill of emotional intelligence and is what normally allows one to remain very composed when handling pressure of any kind. It allows you to calm yourself down during anger and distress and also do the same to other people in the same situation.

Understanding emotions: as an emotionally intelligent person you are also supposed to exercise patience in your reactions and therefore take time to analyze and understand emotions before taking an action. It is exactly what prevents you from being too judgmental and also exercise lenience to yourself and others.

Reasoning with emotions: this makes up for an important part of emotional intelligence and it involves thinking through all our feelings to ensure that we give it a better thought and reaction. It is a skill that allows you to always be a good decision maker and always act out of reason.

Chapter 26: Why My Child Is Abusive?

Have you ever asked this question why my child is abusive? It is a natural process that people always ask 'why' when they found their child behavior highly abusive. Most of the parents feel themselves to be highly responsible for the abusive behavior of their child and they keep themselves blaming. But the actual thing is that there can be very important other things that are contributing to the abusive behavior of your child along with the parental abuse. This includes the abuse of any substance, poor boundaries, some psychological problem, learned behavior or some other similar things.

Most of the children behave violently when they found them to be of poor coping skills, whereas, others enjoy the power to hit their parents. Before starting a complete discussion on the threats and verbal abuse behavior, it is important to consider that these issues are highly difficult to deal with when you are alone in the task. Such type of behavior is a big problem, and the symptoms can be anything that your child is facing. It is entirely the stress for the parents that they have to deal with the abusive child. When considering the abusive child, it is important for the parents to adopt a simple and schematic way to deal with the abusive behavior of their children. Parents should have a structure of guidelines that they should follow to deal with all the serious things that are happening in their home. If you are observing a little problem in your child such as he is resisting for being dressed for school or he is threatening or abusing you verbally, then he is particularly in a big problem.

When your child is abusive to you and your family member, it is important to deal with them on the spot. Make sure that you have clearly told your child that no abuse form will be excused, whether it is physical or any other. Make sure that you are strict with your child as you should clearly tell them you don't need any justifications for abuse and so, you are completely responsible, and there is no excuse now.

Most of the siblings usually tease each other so much frequently and sometimes they are involved in a fight too. These things also come under the abuse as one of the sibling is targeted for the rivalry or demoralizing. You should not consider the teasing and abuse on the same side as they are highly different situations. You have to deal with the matter seriously when you have such things in your home.

Verbal abuse is not a simple thing, and it doesn't go away easily. It has deep roots that have a large impact on your child early development. It is usually some specific time when your child is abusive as a result of some chaos or stress from which he is passing through. They can have some different tone, and they can be very testy. These children cross the line after becoming abusive from the mouth as they shift to the physical abuse that involves the attacking to the people or threatening them. This threatening provides the kids with the power that they should not have at this early stage.

One of the most common reasons for the possession of abusive behavior in the children is that they feel themselves to be completely powerless and in return, they try to gain much more control. Another important reason is that your child might not have enough skills to solve their problem and to deal with all the frustration that they suffer from. They find it hard to cope with the disappointments and the resolution of the matter in a proper way.

This is how such children are unable to develop the social skills or problem-solving skills, including the learning disabilities or family problems a major reason. This is how such kids become the victim of emotion, and they possess uncomfortable skills that become the reason for their inappropriate social behavior. If they don't find any tool to solve their problem, they will remain at the start, and they will further lead to one step forward in the abuse.

Children even abuse their parents too as the power has become the whole solution and this behavior is adopted from his surroundings. Whether it is a video game, music, politics or the movies, these are the potential sources from which your child is gaining aggressive behavior and learning the ways in which he can use his power. Such types of things usually have a strong influence on the teens, and they often think that they lose if they are alone. They are taught to fight when they are young, but they interpret some other meaning, and this fight becomes more intense with time.

Conclusion

The emotional intelligence is important to understand your own emotions and emotions of other people. It is quite beneficial for the individuals to increase self-confidence. You will be able to speak in mind to increase the enthusiasm to fight with different flexible issues and challenges. The emotional intelligence will help you a lot in both personal and professional lives.

The emotional intelligence is also important for the organizations to enhance your confidence. It is important to motivate your employees to work in the favor of organizations and develop unique skills. It enables people to share their creative ideas and build a better relationship with others, including employees, colleagues and clients.

Components of Emotional Intelligence
Various models are introduced to develop strategies and emotional intelligence. One model has four branches and each branch

address a different level of your relationship between logics and emotions. The four branches help you to perceive your emotions and you will be able to understand the meaning of emotions. You should recognize the non-verbal emotional signals. The emotions will help you to understand others and find various outcomes. All branches will help you to strengthen your emotions in a better way, and you can communicate with the world in a better way.

Stress Reduction with Emotional Intelligence

Stress can affect your personal life because you may often take irrational decisions and work against your plans. You should learn to deal with your stress to avoid any trouble, and this can be done in a better way by developing emotional intelligence. It will help you to recognize various stressful situations based on your skills. It enables you to develop your own techniques to reduce stress.

Emotional Awareness with EI

A person should be able to recognize his/her emotions that can affect his/her corporeal and cognitive reactions to the world. Healthy emotional skills are important to develop your ability to recognize different emotions and expression. You should be aware of the effects of emotions and logical thinking for the better utilization of emotions.

Nonverbal Communication Skills

Just like verbal communication, the nonverbal communication is equally important. It may include physical contact, facial expression, vocal tone, postures and eye contact of speakers. Your emotions can greatly affect your emotions and it is important to understand the meanings of your nonverbal expressions. The nonverbal communication can improve your emotional intelligence and enables you to learn and recognize the demonstration of emotions through nonverbal responses.

Learn Humor to Utilize in Your Life

Humor is an important part of your life and it is always considered as the best medicines for your sorrows. Laughter can reduce your stress and enhance your moods. You should learn humor and connect it with emotions to reduce your personal conflicts. Without conflicts, a person will be able to perform well in personal and professional levels to seek alternative solutions for personal as well as social challenges.

Positive Conflict Resolution with Emotional Intelligence

It is not possible to avoid conflicts in your life; therefore, you can learn to resolve your conflicts in a positive way. You can do it easily with the help of emotional intelligence. The stress management has direct link with the expressive feelings and the nonverbal cues as well as humor will help you interact with the world in a better way. Resolve your conflicts in a better way in the four main areas, such as:

Concentration on the current conflict

Arguments

Forgiveness

Unresolved conflicts

CPSIA information can be obtained
at www.ICGtesting.com
Printed in the USA
BVHW041806070720
583060BV00028B/515

9 781989 965252